AMERICA IN PERSPECTIVE

☾

Only his gospel gives us ultimate reasons.
Without such perspective,
we would be like astronomers who have never seen the stars.

*   *   *   *   *

…perspective is precious.

—Neal A. Maxwell

AMERICA IN PERSPECTIVE

LDS PERSPECTIVES ON AMERICA'S PAST, PRESENT, AND FUTURE

Andrew S. Weeks

Writers Club Press

San Jose · New York · Lincoln · Shanghai

America in Perspective

LDS Perspectives on America's Past, Present and Future

Published by Writers Club Press
an imprint of iUniverse.com, Inc.

For information address:
iUniverse.com, Inc.
620 North 48th Street
Suite 201
Lincoln, NE 68504-3467
www.iuniverse.com

ISBN: 0-595-09949-1

Printed in the United States of America

This book is dedicated with love,

To my mother and father, Vivian & Floyd Weeks.
Thank you both for life, and for love,
and for all the good things in between.

&

To my beautiful wife, Heidi.
Thank you for believing in me as well as my dreams.
You truly are my better half.

&

To my son, Brayden Andrew.
You are the future of America. May you always be good to her;
and may she always be kind to you.

Contents

PART II: PERSPECTIVES ON AMERICA'S PRESENT

PART III: PERSPECTIVES ON AMERICA'S FUTURE

Preface
America in Perspective

Love thou thy land—

—Alfred Lord Tennyson

Glorious, hallowed, blessed America!

These are the feelings that arise within me whenever I see the Stars and Stripes fly in the breeze. I have always considered myself patriotic, even as a boy. I recall the feelings I had while a child in elementary school when I learned the words to the song *This Land is Your Land*. A young boy's vision of America screened through my mind and I was proud of my country. I truly felt that this was my land.

I learned patriotism from my parents who allowed the United States flag to fly on the beam of our California home. Much of their patriotism stemmed from service that my father gave in the Korean War. In that bloody conflict my father lost a brother, an uncle I would never know.

When I became of age and made the choice to serve my Heavenly Father on a full-time mission, I was enthralled, as most missionaries are, at receiving my call of service. My assignment was not to serve in exotic Fiji with its paradisiacal islands, nor was I called to serve in historic Germany. Russia had just opened its doors to missionary work, but I was not sent to the Ukraine, or to any foreign land. Instead, I was assigned to labor in the Oklahoma Tulsa Mission, which encompassed the corner areas of the four states: Oklahoma, Kansas, Arkansas, and Missouri. Although it never entered my mind I might serve in what is known as the "Bible belt," after reading my assignment I knew there was reasons for me to serve in Oklahoma. One of the many experiences I had of serving in my homeland was that my patriot feelings rooted even deeper. I was again very proud to be an American citizen and to be enlisted in the Lord's Army, stationed in the great United States.

Yet it wasn't until I returned from my mission that I learned what my obligation was as an American citizen. I came to realize that patriotism is much more than just feelings of pride about one's country. Feelings are only one part of patriotism; civic duty is another.

When I ponder upon America's past I realize what it was that made this country the greatest nation on earth. It was humble reliance on the Divine Hand of Providence; it was a life-style based on wholesome principles; and it was civic duty—a duty to both man and God. It is adherence to these same principles that will keep America strong. If we abandon these ideals, then we abandon America and all that America has stood for for over two hundred years.

There is a book that stands as a monumental work of patriotism that has affected my life deeply and has given me an enduring hope for my beloved country. The book of which I refer is known to the world as the *Book of Mormon.* The Book of Mormon is a companion volume to the Bible and is indeed *Another Testament of Jesus Christ,* for it teaches of Him and His glorious gospel in beauty and simplicity. But some may question, *The Book of Mormon, patriot?* I answer with an emphatic, *Yes!*

Within the pages of the Book of Mormon bold witness is given of the America's being a choice land, highly favored above all others. The Book of Mormon speaks of the blessings available to the nation that reverences the God of the land, which is Jesus Christ. It also gives unmistakable witness to what happens when a nation falls from the pinnacles of grace. Two previous civilizations inhabited the American Continent in times past. Both had destruction awaiting them when they failed to reverence the Lord by ignoring His commandments and shunning His prophets. War was the method imposed upon their wickedness, which eventually swept them to the dust. Book of Mormon prophets warn that the same fate would befall other civilizations that inhabit the land if they also fail to worship the True and Living God. Since the Church's restoration in 1830, prophets and apostles have reiterated time and again the warning given in the Book of Mormon.

But as previously mentioned, I have found an enduring hope for my country through the pages of the Book of Mormon. Although we know through prophetic utterances the trials and tribulations that our generation will have to pass through before millennial times, and much of it with regard to the United States, we can be assured that when Christ comes again the Stars and Stripes will be flying in the breeze over the covenant people of the Lord as they make their refuge in Zion.[1] The ironic thing, however, is that many of the predicted trials and tribulations of the last days concerning our nation does not have to happen. The reason why they will happen, as foretold by prophets, is because the people as a whole will not turn to the Lord as they ought. In essence, the nation we know today as the United States of America is following the dictates of carnality—the same as the Jaredites and Nephites before them.

---

[1]   See Ezra Taft Benson, *The Constitution: A Heavenly Banner*, p. 33; hereafter cited as *Banner*.

Yet we have responsibility. Ultimately, as James A. Michener wrote, it is up to us to "delay the decline."[2] To help do this, "We must become responsible citizens and carry out our civic duty. We should be 'anxiously engaged' in good causes and leave the world a better place for having lived in it."[3]

---

2   *This Noble Land: My Vision for America*, p. 239; hereafter cited as *This Noble Land*.

Bishop Glenn L. Pace said in the October 1990 General Conference that "we need to overcome fatalism. We know the prophecies of the future. We know the final outcome. We know the world collectively will not repent, and, consequently, the last days will be filled with much pain and suffering. Therefore, we could throw up our hands and do nothing but pray for the end to come so the millennial reign could begin. To do so would forfeit our right to participate in the grand event we are all awaiting. *We must all become players in the winding up scene, not spectators. We must do all we can to prevent calamities* and then do everything possible to assist and comfort the victims of tragedies that do occur.

Lehi set an excellent example for us in the way he handled his knowledge relative to the future of Laman and Lemuel. Early in their lives, Lehi had a vision that disclosed Laman and Lemuel would not partake of the fruit of the tree of life. Immediately after the vision, however, 'he did exhort them...with all the feeling of a tender parent, that they would hearken to his words, that perhaps the Lord would be merciful to them.' (1 Nephi 8:37). During the remainder of Lehi's life, Laman and Lemuel's actions gave him little hope that they would repent. However, he never gave up but labored with them and loved them even with his dying breath (see 2 Nephi 1:21).

The great prophet Mormon set another example worthy of emulation. He lived at a time that was hopeless. Imagine this: 'There were no gifts from the Lord, and the Holy Ghost did not come upon any, because of their wickedness and unbelief' (Mormon 1:14).

In spite of this hopeless situation, Mormon lead their armies, for, in his words, 'Notwithstanding their wickedness I...loved them, according to the love of God which was in me, with all my heart; and my soul had been poured out in prayer unto my God all the day long for them' (Mormon 3:12).

This prophet had Christlike love for a fallen people. Can we be content with loving less? We must press forward with the pure love of Christ to spread the good news of the gospel. As we do so and fight the war of good against evil, light against darkness, and truth against falsehood, we must not neglect our responsibility of dressing the wounds of those who have fallen in battle. There is no room in the kingdom for fatalism" (*Conference Report* October, 1990, p. 8; hereafter cited as *CR*).

3   Ezra Taft Benson, as quoted in *The Spirit of America: Patriotic Speeches from America's Freedom Festival*, p. 9; hereafter cited as *The Spirit of America*.

Why Another Book on American Themes?

The title of this book was decided upon during the evolutionary phases of the manuscript. As you can see, it is not a big book. It is not a history book. It is not a comprehensive book. So many more topics could be included in this book, but they are purposefully lacking. The topics covered, however, deal with crucial themes concerning America's past, present, and future as seen through an LDS perspective of them. Thus it is written mainly for the LDS audience, yet simply enough that others not familiar with LDS doctrine may understand the narrative.

America in Perspective is not meant in any way to downplay the United States by reiterating social problems, government ruin, or other dilemmas confronting American society. This has been done countless times in numerous books and pamphlets. Whereas these themes do have a place in part two of this book, *America in Perspective* has a larger, more ideal ambition.[4] President Harold B. Lee once counseled his brethren of the Twelve:

> While it is true there are dangers and difficulties that lie ahead of us, we must not assume that we are going to stand by and watch the country go to ruin. We should not be heard to predict ills and calamities for the nation. On the contrary, we should be providing optimistic support for the nation.... We must tell the world how we feel about this land and this nation and should bear our testimonies about the great mission and destiny that it has.... We must be careful that we do not say or do anything that will further weaken the country. It is the negative, pessimistic comments about the nation that do as much harm as anything to the country today.[5]

---

4   Patrick Henry said on March 23, 1775, "different men often see the same subject in different lights."

5   *The Teachings of Harold B. Lee*, p. 366; hereafter cited as *THBL*.

I agree with President Lee. There is enough depression in the world without having to elicit and explain in detailed re-hash the problems we face in today's crucial times. It would be naïve of us, however, if we ignored our problems, and even more foolish if we did nothing to help overcome them. Iteration of current and alleged problems has to be assimilated to a certain degree, for as Abraham Lincoln wisely taught: "If we could first know where we are, and whither we are tending, we could better judge what to do, and how to do it." Intelligently then, "We must awake to a sense of our situation and raise a voice of warning." Fortunately, however, the warning voice "need not be one of hopelessness nor of doom. *We do have hope and we have great promise.*"[6] This is the general theme of the book.

Thus in the truest sense, *America in Perspective* is not as much a book about what's wrong with America as it is about what's right with America. The book's overall summation is this: Yes, trials await our America, but so do blessings. Much decay is rotting the fabric of society, and in many ways we are not the nation we used to be. But no, America will not go to hell. We, the citizens of this noble land, and especially the members of The Church of Jesus Christ of Latter-day Saints, have great (if not grave) responsibility. If only by the elders of Israel, the Constitutional principles of freedom and integrity will be preserved. We will let that light shine in Zion. And that is glorious news!

Noted author, Duane S. Crowther has written: "The United States of America is truly a land of freedom [and countless blessings]. It is a nation with a great heritage, an inspiring history, *and the potential for a glorious future.*"[7] Ultimately, I believe in the goodness of the American dream—the potential for a glorious future. However, far too many people have let that dream die within them, harboring such feelings as, "What's the us?" Yet we must remember our obligation is fixed: One person does make a difference.

---

6   Robert E. Hales, *Secret Combinations Today: A Voice of Warning*, p. 13; emphasis added.
7   *America: God's Chosen Land of Liberty*, p. 42; emphasis added.

The story is told of a young man who walked along a beautiful beach at high tide. In the distance he saw an older man who would numerous times bend down and pick objects off the golden sand, then throw the objets into the sea. As the young man approached he noticed the objects which the old man was throwing into the sea were starfish. "What are you doing, old man?" he asked. The old man replied, "I am trying to save these stranded, helpless starfish. You see," the old man continued, "if somebody doesn't help them get back into the ocean where they belong, they will die." The young man shook his head in disbelief and debated. "But sir," he said, "there are countless beaches in the world with thousands of starfish washed to shore, helpless and dying. There is no possible way that you can make a difference. For you cannot walk all the beaches of the world and save all dying starfish!" The old man looked out as far as he could see, where water and sky met. The sun would soon sink below the horizon, and with its sinking strike the soft colors of pink and orange across the eternal sky. Then of a sudden the old man bent over and picked a starfish off the sand, the largest he had seen that day, and with conviction hurled it out to sea as far as he could throw. "There," the old man said, "I just made a difference in that starfish's life!"

Edmund Burke once said: "All that is necessary for the triumph of evil is that good men do nothing." This book, however meager it may be, is my attempt to *do something*.

Perhaps I as the writer have learned more through the writing of this book than what the reader ever will from it. Maybe this is as it should be. But I hope *America in Perspective* will prompt the same feelings to you as you read it, as I had while writing it. Those feelings are empathetic to gratitude for the past, courage for the present, and hope for the future. If the book does this, then its creation has not been in vain.

It is my prayer that we put anxiety away and develop the faith that is equal to or greater than the days ahead; that we be people of courage and conviction, being honorable citizens and doing what we can to preserve the integrity of our noble land; that we glean from eyes of understanding and see America in the true light of our Father's Plan—the role she has played, now plays, and will yet play in His divine drama. And let us be grateful that we, too, are part of American history and part of the Father's Plan.

The Church and Politics

President Spencer W. Kimball cautioned church members to "avoid...involving the Church in political issues. It is so easy," he said, "if we are not careful, to project our personal preferences as the position of the Church on an issue."[8] Although the very nature of this book deals with American issues and prophetic statements, how they are used in the manuscript is the author's doing. And although I have sought diligently to be harmony with the teachings of the brethren, the conclusions drawn are my own. This book is a private endeavor and I alone am responsible for the content. Emphatically I say, this is *not* a Church publication.

For any mistakes or wrong conclusions found within the pages of this book, I assume complete responsibility. For the good found herein let the honor be given to not the author of the work, but the Giver of the gifts, our Heavenly Father.

---

[8]   *The Teachings of Spencer W. Kimball*, p. 406; hereafter cited as *TSWK*.

Acknowledgements

Though this book is a private endeavor, there are undoubtedly a few individuals I wish to acknowledge here. First, I want to thank my wife, Heidi, for whom this book is dedicated. She has been a source of strength, inspiration, and encouragement to me during this writing project and many others. She sees in me what I often cannot see in myself, and I am grateful that she fell in love with a dreamer.

I also want to thank my mother and father, Vivian and Floyd Weeks, to whom also this work is dedicated. Their love and support in many ways has been full, even to overflowing. Thank you both for believing in my abilities, and for teaching me the values I have tried to exemplify in this work.

Special thanks go out to many family members for encouraging me with kind words to proceed with and accomplish my writing goals. Once while talking on his front porch late on a summer's eve, my brother encouraged me, saying in essence: "Keep plugging away. One day you'll make it happen!" Though I haven't *made it happen* yet, this book is a definitive start.

I wish to also thank Craig Nytch, one of my best friends and a true brother in the gospel. Though this book does not have his name on the dedication page, the work was originally inspired through the lengthy and energetic conversations we have shared together over the years related to the American theme. A greater patriot I have not known, and I dare say, nor this country. I cannot help but think of these scriptural words when I think of my friend, Craig: "If all men had been, and were, and ever would be, like unto [Craig Nytch], behold, the very powers of hell would have been shaken forever" (Alma 48:17).

Part I:

PERSPECTIVES ON
AMERICA'S   PAST

No man, however brilliant and perceptive,
shall have a complete understanding of our nation's history
without this knowledge and conviction....
The real story of America is one that shows the hand of God
in our nation's beginning.

—Ezra Taft Benson

1

A Choice Land

[The Lord] leadeth away the righteous into precious lands...

—1 Nephi 17:38

Pangaea, Eden, and America

When the earth was first created, it was much different than it is today. This is obvious. The time lapse of centuries, including nature's upheavals, has done much to alter the geographical landscape of planet earth. In its infant days the earth had only one landmass, a condition known as Pangaea.[1] In this state there was no division of continents as we now have.

---

[1]   Named by the German meteorologist, Alfred Wegener, who postulated that a massive supercontinent existed about 200 million years ago.

It wasn't until after the waters abated during the great deluge of Noah's time that the geographical puzzle was dispersed across the globe.[2]

It was in the center place of Pangaea where our first parents, Adam and Eve, lived. They enjoyed their abode in a lush garden east of a place called Eden (see Genesis 2:8; Moses 3:8, 15; Abraham. 5:8, 11). Revelation given in modern times explain that Eden bordered in what now is known as North America. Brigham Young related the following: "Joseph, the Prophet, told me that the Garden of Eden was in Jackson County, Missouri. When Adam was driven out [of the garden] he went to the place we now call Adam-ondi-Ahman, Daviess County, Missouri. There he built an altar and offered sacrifices."[3] This truth clarifies a popular misconception: the cradle of the world was not in the Eastern Hemisphere as many falsely suppose, but rather the Western Hemisphere encompassing what now is called the United States of America. A popular hymn written by William W. Phelps reflects the drama of Eden in these words:

---

[2]   The Bible states that it was in the days of Peleg that the earth was divided (see Genesis 10:25). President Joseph Fielding Smith explained that "The dividing of the earth was not an act of division by the inhabitants of the earth by tribes and peoples, but a breaking asunder of the continents, thus dividing the land surface and creating the Eastern Hemisphere and Western Hemisphere. By looking at a wall map of the world, you will discover how the land surface along the northern and southern coast of the American Hemisphere and Europe and Africa has the appearance of having been together at one time. Of course, there have been many changes on the earth's surface since the beginning. We are informed by revelation that the time will come when this condition will be changed and that the land surface of the earth will come back again as it was in the beginning and all be in one place [see Doctrine & Covenants 133:18-20]." (*Answers to Gospel Questions*, Vol. 5, pp. 73-74.)

[3]   As quoted in *The Man Adam*, p. 20. See also D&C 117:8 and D&C 107:53.

This earth was once a garden place,
With all her glories common,
And men did live a holy race,
And worship Jesus face to face
In Adam-ondi-Ahman

*   *   *   *   *

Her land was good and greatly blest,
Beyond all Israel's Canaan;
Her fame was known from east to west,
Her peace was great and pure the rest
Of Adam-ondi-Ahman[4]

It is not fiction or fantasy but in every way reality that the ancients knew this land well. They beheld its rugged mountains and rolling hills, as their cattle grazed in its green pastures. They fished its streams and hunted its forests; they built cities such as Nod and multiplied to enormous proportions. They toiled, sacrificed, and worshipped Jehovah on its soil. It was here that God first communed with man; and it was here that man first sinned. Perhaps these ancients even sang a battle hymn, much like our own national anthem. The patriarchs called the land Zion[5], and

---

4   *Hymns of The Church of Jesus Christ of Latter-day Saints,* hymn #49.
5   The word *Zion* has multiple meanings. An explanation of its use in this book is here given: *The Land of Zion* refers to the lands of North and South America generally and to the United States specifically. *The City of Zion* (New Jerusalem) refers to the future city the saints will build in Jackson County, Missouri, prior to the advent of Christ. Other uses of the word *Zion* refer to *the pure in heart* and the *righteous membership of the Church,* including its stakes, wards, temples, and other places of refuge. The intent of use in this book is readily apparent (see also the LDS Bible Dictionary under *Zion*).

to the pure in heart America has always been such. "The whole of America," explained Joseph Smith, "from north to south...is...Zion." This is where the "mountain of the Lord [will] be." Furthermore the Prophet noted, "When the Elders shall take up and examine the Bible, they will see it."[6]

The Bible does give slight reference to specific Zions that have existed on this continent in time's past. For instance, Enoch's city of Zion was somewhere in Pangaea (Moses 7:17-19). A very plausible assertion is that it was within the borders now known as North America. The Bible corresponds with latter-day revelation and tells of a New Jerusalem that is to be constructed in the last days, or millennial era, patterned after old Jerusalem (see Isaiah 1:27, 2:3, 4:3-5, 33:20; Jeremiah 3:14, 31:6; Obadiah 1:17; see also Articles of Faith 10; Ether 13:4, 8 [2-12]; D&C 45:65-71; Moses 7:62). Thus from the primeval days of Adam's garden Zion to the future New Jerusalem, the land of America, known to prophets and saints as *Zion*, has and will yet play crucial roles in the divine purposes of the Lord.

The Tower of Babel and the Coming of the Jaredites

We read in the Old Testament that approximately between 3000 BC and 2200 BC the idolatrous people of Israel sought heaven's glory through a makeshift tower built in Babylon and which, as Josephus records, was constructed "too high for the waters to...reach," if God "should have a mind to drown the world again."[7] This display of incredulity so displeased

---

6   *Teachings of the Prophet Joseph Smith*, p. 362; hereafter cited as *TPJS*.
7   *Antiquities of the Jews* IV:2.

the Lord that He said, "Behold…now nothing will be restrained from them, which they have imagined to do. [I will go down] and there confound their language, that they may not understand one another's speech." The historic drama follows:

> So the Lord scattered them abroad from thence upon the face of all the earth; and they left off to build the city. Therefore is the name of it called Babel; because the Lord did there confound the language of all the earth: and from thence did the Lord scatter them abroad upon the face of all the earth (Genesis 11:6-9).

Historian Flavius Josephus has abridged for us the same account, saying:

> When God saw that they acted so madly, he did not resolve to destroy them utterly, since they were not grown wiser by the destruction of the former sinners; but he caused a tumult among them, by producing in them divers languages; and causing that, through the multitude of those languages, they should not be able to understand one another. The place wherein they built the tower is now called Babylon; because of the confusion of that language which they readily understood before; for the Hebrews mean by the word Babel, Confusion.[8]

What the Old Testament and Josephus fail to mention, however, is that during Babel's time there were some that were spared the confusion of tongues. But alas, through the blessing of restoration scripture we do have a better understanding of what took place during this crucial time in history's long past, including who these chosen people were who were spared the mass confusion and scattering.

---

[8]   Ibid. IV:3

The Book of Mormon is the pivotal account concerning this time period, that tells of a man whose name was Jared, who had a brother that was humble, righteous, and "highly favored of the Lord" (Ether 1:34), and who is known in the sacred record only as "the brother of Jared." Jared, knowing the standing his brother held with the Lord, said to him: "Cry unto the Lord, that he will not confound us that we may not understand our words."

> And it came to pass that the brother of Jared did cry unto the Lord, and the Lord had compassion upon Jared; therefore he did not confound the language of Jared; and Jared and his brother was not confounded.
>
> Then Jared said unto his brother: Cry again unto the Lord, and it may be that he will turn away his anger from them who are our friends, that he confound not their language.
>
> And it came to pass that the brother of Jared did cry unto the Lord, and the Lord had compassion upon their friends and their families also, that they were not confounded.
>
> And it came to pass that Jared spake again unto his brother, saying: Go and inquire of the Lord whether he will drive us out of the land, and if he will drive us out of the land, cry unto him whither we shall go. And who knoweth but the Lord will carry us forth into a land which is choice above all the earth? And if it so be, let us be faithful unto the Lord, that we may receive it for our inheritance.
>
> And it came to pass that the brother of Jared did cry unto the Lord according to that which had been spoken by the mouth of Jared.
>
> And it came to pass that the Lord did hear the brother of Jared, and had compassion upon him, and said unto him:
>
> Go to and gather together thy flocks, both male and female, of every kind; and thy families; and also Jared thy brother and his family; and also thy friends and their families, and the friends of Jared and their families.

And when thou hast done this thou shalt go at the head of them down into the valley which is northward. And there will I meet thee, and I will go before thee into a land which is choice above all other lands of the earth.

And there will I bless thee and thy seed, and raise up unto me of thy seed, and of the seed of thy brother, and they who shall go with thee, a great nation (Ether 1:34-43).

Sailing barges were constructed which took them across the mighty ocean. After almost a year at sea Jared, his brother, and their families and friends set foot on the "Americas." It was a beautiful land to them, full of milk and honey, a land of ore and wild beasts, of hope and promises. Fulfilling ancient custom of naming themselves after their primal leaders (see 1 Nephi 3:5 [6-10]), the people became known as the Jaredites. And just like the patriarchal fathers did before them, the Jaredites toiled, sacrificed, and worshipped in the land of Zion. They multiplied and replenished the land. And fulfilling the promises of the Lord, they became a "great nation" politically, economically, and militarily (see Ether 6:18, 28; 7:20). For generations they waxed strong in righteousness and peace (Ether 6:17; 7:25-27). Eventually, however, as does happen when people replace God with mammon, pride enveloped the people and secret combinations destroyed the government (Ether 8:13-26, 9:26). Chaos and war ensued (Ether 11:7), which eventually exterminated the whole of the Jaredite nation (Ether 9:12; 13-15). A later civilization that inhabited the Americas found a deserted valley of dry bones (Omni 1:20-22; Mosiah 8:8; 21:26-27; Alma 22:30; see also Ether 11:6) and called it the "land of desolation." The haunting memory of the place bespoke of sin and death. It was there that the final battles of the once great nation of Jaredites were fought (Ether 13-15). Jaredite prophet and historian, Ether, left behind an historical as well as religious record concerning his people. Moroni later abridged Ether's record into his own, and Joseph Smith translated it as part of the Book of Mormon, which was published to the world in 1830 as *Another Testament of Jesus Christ.*

The Seed of Joseph

While the greatest insight into the validity of America being a choice land comes from latter-day scripture, the Holy Bible does hint at it.

The Old Testament records the patriarch Jacob giving his son a blessing, which said: "Joseph is a fruitful bough, even a fruitful bough by a well; whose branches run over the wall." Analyzing these words, the fruitful bough spoken of is the posterity that would spring from Joseph's loins as part of the Abrahamic Covenant. The wall referred to is Jerusalem's wall. What the patriarch was telling his son was that Joseph's posterity would become so many that they would literally "run over the wall," meaning a portion of them would leave the confines of Jerusalem, or more precisely Israel. A well holds water. Could it be that the well referred to was the ocean? In this context, a remnant of Joseph's posterity would leave Israel and travel the ocean to other lands.

Jacob also prophesied upon the head of his son: "The head of thy father have prevailed above the blessings of my progenitors *unto the utmost bound of the everlasting hills: they shall be on the head of Joseph*, and on the crown of the head of *him that was separate from his brethren*" (Genesis 49:22-26). The father was foretelling his son that a remnant of his (Joseph's) seed would be separated from that of his brethren (the other Tribes) who remained in Israel, even unto the "utmost bound of the everlasting hills."[9]

---

[9] Apostle Orson Pratt explained that "the term *utmost bound* must have reference to the most distant portions of the earth. The geographical position of America corresponds, as to distance, with the terms of the prophecy. The range of mountains extending the whole length of the great western continent, are the longest in the whole world, and may well be designated by the Prophet Jacob as the *everlasting hills*" (Orson Pratt's Works, p. 281).

Without the revealed stick of Joseph (see Ezekiel 37:15-17, 19; Nephi 3:12 [7-15]) we would never know the full meaning of this wonderful prophetic blessing. But thankfully we do have the stick of Joseph that contains the message of Nephi, which says: "...it sufficeth me to say that we are the descendants of Joseph" (1 Nephi 6:2).

Nephites, Lamanites, and the Land of Promise

We learn of Nephi, a native of Jerusalem, from his own narrative beginning in 600 BC (circa). Zedekiah reigned as King of Judah. The people of Israel were apostate and wicked. Nephi tells us that the Lord called "many prophets" at this time to warn the people that if they did not repent their great city Jerusalem would be destroyed (1 Nephi 1:4; 2 Kings 17:13-15; 2 Chronicles 36:15-16; Jeremiah 7:25; 26:20). The Lord warned that their oppressors, the Babylonians, would take those who escaped death captive. The pages of history teach that Israel did not repent and the oppressors came.

One of the many prophets who raised the voice of warning was Lehi, Nephi's father, whose ancestry came from Jacob's son, Joseph. Calling a whole city to repentance is not an easy thing to do, especially since "the guilty taketh the truth to be hard" (1 Nephi 16:2). Instead of heeding the warning calls of the prophets of God, the people sought to kill the prophets, including Lehi (1 Nephi 1:20).

During midnight hours, Lehi, having been warned that his life was in jeopardy, took leave of Jerusalem (1 Nephi 2:1-5), and with his family, entrusted their care to the promises of the Lord, which said: "inasmuch as ye shall keep my commandments, ye shall prosper, and shall be lead to a land of promise; yea, even a land which is choice above all other lands" (1 Nephi 2:20). Others eventually joined Lehi's mission. They lived and journeyed in the "wilderness" of Israel for nearly eight years, much of the time near the boarders of the Red Sea. Finally, under directions from the

Lord travel arrangements were made and this small group of wanderers, outcasts of Jerusalem, embarked on the mighty ocean, sailing to somewhere unbeknown to Lehi and his clan.

We learn of these things from Nephi, the first of Book of Mormon authors. Nephi's record states that Lehi and his following arrived in the Promised Land in 589 BC (circa). It was a New World to them, yet it was as old as mankind. With ecstatic yet humble delight, Lehi proclaimed the land to be "a land for the inheritance of my seed. Yea, the Lord hath covenanted this land unto me," he said, "and to my children forever, and also all those who would be lead out of other countries by the hand of the Lord" (2 Nephi 1:15). Such has been the promise, and such has been its literal fulfillment: countless millions have been "lead out of other countries," and have found refuge in the land of Zion (see 1 Nephi 13:13-20).

It wasn't long after arriving in the land of promise that Lehi died. But before he did he gathered his family together and admonished them in the ways of righteousness. He praised his two younger sons, Nephi and Sam, for being obedient to the counsels and commandments of God, and for their great desire to do what was right. He plead and warned his two elder sons, Laman and Lemuel, who had always been quick to doubt and disobey, to follow the example of Nephi and Sam. But envy and malice were in the hearts of Laman and Lemuel, and shortly after Lehi died they sought to take away the life of their younger brother, Nephi. This intent was quickly made known to Nephi, however, who took his immediate family, including Sam, and fled into other regions of the American continent (2 Nephi 5:5).

For their wickedness an eventual curse of black skins came upon the posterity of Laman and Lemuel (2 Nephi 5:20-23), who by this time were known as Lamanites (2 Nephi 5:14). Nephi and his followers became known as the Nephites (2 Nephi 5:9), and for their righteousness retained the fairness of their skins.

While the Nephites multiplied and prospered in industry, economics, and righteousness, the Lamanites grew more degenerate and apostate, even at times turning to a form of cannibalism. There was an epoch where the setting was reversed, however, and the Lamanites sought the Lord while the Nephites forsook Him. In fact, one of the great messages of the Book of Mormon is that great nations can "fall from grace." The conclusive effort of the Book of Mormon tells of the final conflict between the Nephites and Lamanites (Mormon 1-6). In the end, both nations had forsaken the God of the land, which is Jesus Christ. They had broken the covenant as given to Lehi a thousand years earlier (see 2 Nephi 1:5-12). Like the Jaredites before them, the once great nation of Nephites was utterly destroyed at Cumorah in AD 421 (circa). The covenant the Lord made to Lehi and his posterity close to three thousand years ago remains intact for those who live in Zion today.[10]

America during the Time of Christ

Most of Christendom regard Palestine as the Holy Land because it is the place where the Son of God lived. However, while it is true that Christ walked the dusty roads of Galilee, it is also true that He who is no respecter of persons walked the fruitful plains of the American Continent. After explaining to the Jews that He was the Good Shepherd and knew His sheep, the Savior said: "And other sheep I have which are not of this fold. Them also I must bring, and they shall hear my voice; and there shall be one fold and one shepherd" (John 10:16). Many modern Christianists assume He made reference to the Gentiles, who as yet did not have the

---

[10] "Herein is our security: *so long as the people of America will serve the God of this land, who is Jesus Christ, no power on earth shall overcome her or conquer her.* In modern revelation it is said that the wicked inhabitants of the earth will say, 'Let us not go to battle against Zion, because her inhabitants are terrible.' Zion *is* America" (*Sermons and Missionary Services of Melvin J. Ballard*, p. 267; emphasis added). The Lord warned in our day: "beware of pride, lest ye become like the Nephites of old" (D&C 38:39).

gospel preached to them. Yet this belief is false, for Christ declared: "I am not sent but unto the lost sheep of the house of Israel" (Matthew 15:24). The question is then left: *Who were the other sheep of whom Christ referred?*

That Prophet of great stature, Nephi, who was desirous to behold the things which his father had seen (1 Nephi 11:1-6), was given a marvelous vision concerning his people, including the coming of Christ and a visitation He would make to Nephi's posterity in the new world. Nephi's vision dramatized chaos among his people, including the destructive forces of nature that would precede Messiah's coming.

> And it came to pass...I looked and beheld the land of promise; and I beheld multitudes of people, yea, even as it were in number as many as the sand of the sea.
>
> And it came to pass that I beheld multitudes gathered together to battle, one against the other; and I beheld wars, and rumors of wars, and great slaughters with the sword among my people.
>
> And it came to pass that I beheld many generations pass away, after the manner of wars and contentions in the land; and I beheld many cities, yea, even I did not number them all.
>
> And it came to pass that I saw a mist of darkness on the face of the land of promise; and I saw lightnings, and I heard thunderings, and earthquakes, and all manner of tumultuous noises; and I saw the earth and the rocks, that they rent; and I saw mountains tumbling into pieces; and I saw the plains of the earth, that they were broken up; and I saw many cities that they were sunk; and I saw many that they were burned with fire; and I saw many that did tumble to the earth, because of the quaking thereof.
>
> And it came to pass after I saw these things, I saw the vapor of darkness, that it passed from off the face of the earth; and behold, I saw multitudes who had not fallen because of the great and terrible judgements of the Lord (1 Nephi 12:1-5).

While this was Nephi's testimony of a then future event, a later Nephi recorded it after it happened (see 3 Nephi 8-10). Nephi's vision pinnacled this event: "And I saw the heavens open, and the Lamb of God descending out of heaven; and he came down and showed himself unto [my seed]" (1 Nephi 12:6). The drama itself is enacted as follows:

> And now it came to pass that there were a great multitude gathered together, of the people of Nephi, round about the temple which was in the land Bountiful; and they were marveling and wondering one with another, and were showing one to another the great and marvelous change which had taken place....
>
> And it came to pass that while they were thus conversing one with another, they heard a voice as if it came out of heaven; and they cast their eyes round about, for they understood not the voice which they heard; and it was not a harsh voice, neither was it a loud voice; nevertheless, and notwithstanding it being a small voice it did pierce them that did hear to the center, insomuch that there was no part of their frame that it did not cause to quake; yea, it did pierce them to the very soul, and did cause their hearts to burn.
>
> And it came to pass that again they heard the voice, and they understood it not.
>
> And again the third time they did hear the voice, and did open their ears to hear it; and their eyes were toward the sound thereof; and they did look steadfastly towards heaven, from whence the sound came.
>
> And behold, the third time they did understand the voice which they heard; and it said unto them:
>
> Behold my Beloved Son, in whom I am well pleased, in whom I have glorified my name—hear ye him.
>
> And it came to pass, as they understood they cast their eyes up again towards heaven; and behold, they saw a Man descending out of heaven; and he was clothed in a white robe; and he came down

and stood in the midst of them; and the eyes of the whole multitude were turned upon him, and they durst not open their mouths, even one to another, and wist not what it meant, for they thought it was an angel that had appeared unto them.

And it came to pass that he stretched forth his hand and spake unto the people, saying: Behold, I am Jesus Christ, whom the prophets testified shall come into the world (3 Nephi 11:1-10).

This is the crowning event in the Book of Mormon. Christ came to the Nephites soon after His resurrection in Jerusalem. Stories of the great white-bearded God, Quetzaquatal, are in the historic annals of the Aztec and Maya legends, whose ancestors are the Lamanites. But it is the sacred text of the Book of Mormon to which we turn to learn sound doctrine. Through this sacred text we understand who the other sheep were of whom Christ referred. For to the Nephites He testified: "ye are they of whom I said: Other sheep I have which are not of this fold; them also I must bring, and they shall hear my voice; and there shall be one fold and one shepherd…behold, ye have both heard my voice, and seen me; and ye are my sheep, and ye are numbered among those whom the Father hath given me" (3 Nephi 15:21, 24 [12-24]). Thus we learn the Savior of the world came not only to the Jews of Jerusalem, but also to the seed of Joseph on the American continent, teaching His gospel to this portion of the House of Israel who made their home in the land of promise.

From Columbus to Plymouth Rock

Looking at still another epoch of American history, and doing so with doctrinal background, we turn again to that wonderful prophetic vision of Nephi, who beheld "a man among the Gentiles…and he went forth upon the many waters, even unto the seed of my brethren, who were in the promised land" (1 Nephi 13:12). Nephi's prophecy is now but history;

it has all come to pass, every jot and tittle. The man whom Nephi beheld through the vista of revelation was no more nor less than Christopher Columbus, who in 1492 set foot a lost world inhabited only by decadent natives.

Concerning Columbus' voyage, Nephi makes it clear that the navigator was influenced by the Spirit of God to undertake such a venture: "the Spirit of God...came down and wrought upon the man." Reflecting on his mission, Columbus himself testified: "Our Lord unlocked my mind, sent me upon the sea, and gave me fire for the deed. Those who heard of my emprise called it foolish, mocked me, and laughed. But who can doubt but that the Holy Ghost inspired me?"[11]

Nephi's account brings a whole new perspective—a spiritual perspective—to Columbus and our Pilgrim fathers than what contemporary history buffs would teach. The American theme was written long ago in the annals of prophecy and revelation. Even before the Pilgrims landed at Plymouth Rock the destiny of this land was already decided. President Ezra Taft Benson wrote:

> The destiny of America was divinely decreed.... As in an enacted drama, the players who came on the scene were rehearsed and selected for their parts.... As one looks back on what we call our history, there is a telling theme that occurs again and again in this drama. It is that God governs in the affairs of this nation.[12]

Much of the earth's historic past as well as its future were enacted in vision for Nephi, who in turn was commanded to write what he saw. The record we have from this obedient son of Lehi is prophecy unmolested. As

---

11 As quoted in Ezra Taft Benson, *This Nation Shall Endure*, p. 13.
12 Ibid. p. 11.

we continue reading his account, we learn that he saw the "Spirit of God...wrought upon other Gentiles," after which "went forth out of captivity upon the many waters," eventually arriving in the "land of promise; and I beheld the wrath of God," said Nephi, "that it was upon the seed of my brethren; and they were scattered before the Gentiles and were smitten."

> And I beheld the Spirit of the Lord, that it was upon the Gentiles, and they did prosper and obtain the land for their inheritance; and I beheld that they were white, and exceedingly fair and beautiful, like unto my people before they were slain.
>
> And it came to pass that I, Nephi, beheld that the Gentiles who had gone forth out of captivity did humble themselves before the Lord; and the power of the Lord was with them.
>
> And I beheld that their mother Gentiles were gathered together upon the many waters, and upon the land also, to battle against them.
>
> And I beheld that the power of God was with them, and also that the wrath of God was upon all those that were gathered together against them to battle.
>
> And I, Nephi, beheld that the Gentiles that had gone out of captivity were delivered by the power of God out of the hands of all other nations.
>
> And it came to pass that I, Nephi, beheld that they did prosper in the land; and I beheld a book, and it was carried forth among them (1 Nephi 13:12-20).

Not only does holy writ attest that "Gentiles" fled their native lands to find refuge and prosperity on the American continent but so do our history books, with ample verification of Nephi's prophecy. In retrospect, we know who these "Gentiles" were of whom Nephi spoke—the Colonizers who took flight from European oppression. Notice that Nephi "beheld a book, and it was carried forth among them." The Colonizers were God-fearing men and women who relied on the teachings of the Bible as their great moral standard. As they honored heaven, heaven honored them and granted them victory over their "mother Gentiles." Concerning such a remarkable victory, President Ezra Taft Benson said of the colonists: "From the standpoint of numbers, equipment, training, and resources the rag-tag army of the colonists should never have won the war for independence. But America's destiny was not to be determined by overwhelming numbers, or better military weapons, or strategy.... God took a direct hand in the events that led to the defeat of the British."[13]

Nephi's vision, as glorious as it must have been for him, must have been difficult for the prophet to behold. For it was revealed that his descendants would become degenerate, eventually being "scattered" and "smitten" by the white man. This is the tragedy of the whole drama. "Inasmuch as ye shall keep my commandments," the Lord repeated time and again, "ye shall prosper." Otherwise, He warned, "ye shall be cut off from my presence" (2 Nephi 4:4; see also 1 Nephi 2:20-21; Alma 9:13). Such has been the blessing and the cursing related to the Promised Land from the dawn of time. Conditions are to be met, restrictions imposed. The promises of the Lord are sure; so are His warnings.

---

[13] As quoted in *The Spirit of America*, p. 3.

Brigham Young said: "Through the power of Almighty God, and in accordance with the words of the Lord, as contained in the Book of Mormon, [the Colonists] were, in the first place, impelled to come here, and after coming here, to contend for human freedom upon this land."[14] And President George Albert Smith confirmed, "It was the Lord that inspired that little band of people who crossed the mighty ocean and landed at Plymouth Rock, because they desired to worship him according to the dictates of their own conscience. He watched over them and safeguarded their descendants and those who followed them to America, and in due time, there came an opportunity to establish liberty such as humankind had not known before."[15]

Indeed, the Lord *is* merciful and kind and "created the earth that it should be inhabited; and he hath created his children that they should possess it.... *And he leadeth away the righteous into precious lands*" (1 Nephi 17:38, emphasis added).

---

[14] *Journal of Discourses* 24:126; hereafter cited as *JD*.
[15] *The Teachings of George Albert Smith* p. 166; hereafter cited as *TGAS*.

2
The American Constitution—
An Inspired Document

Let [the Constitution] be taught in schools, in seminaries, and in colleges,
let it be written in primers, in spelling books and almanacs,
let it be preached from the pulpit, proclaimed in legislative halls,
and enforced in courts of justice.
And, in short, let it become the political religion of the nation.

—Abraham Lincoln

History in Brief

It has been over two hundred years since George Washington and other remembered men of integrity signed the document that insured to America and her citizens their freedom. That document was put into effect to form a "more perfect union." Whereas for many years the original thirteen colonies enjoyed their first Constitution, *The Articles of*

Confederation, "The document read more like a treaty between nations [rather] than a device to link component states."[1] While absence of sufficient power in the central government was one of the *Articles'* deficiencies, too much power granted to individual states was another. "Local majorities unchecked by national power, could infringe individual rights."[2] These and other concerns lead to a reformation of the *Articles*, making possible the creation of the United States Constitution, which was signed into agreement on September 17, 1787. Ratification came in 1789.[3]

The Hand That Framed It

The Constitution of the United States is akin to scripture, in that, it too was inspired by Deity and has His mark of approval. Speaking in this vein, President Ezra Taft Benson expressed these sentiments: "I reverence the Constitution of the United States as a sacred document. To me its words are akin to the revelations of God, for God has placed His stamp of approval on the Constitution of this land."[4] This is a theme that every prophet has emphasized when speaking of the Constitution: that God inspired it. In his day President George Albert Smith said: "I am saying to

---

[1] *American Government*, 2d edition, p. 24.

[2] Ibid. p. 27.

[3] "The Constitution as signed lacked a Bill of Rights, though these rights were discussed in the Convention. As the Colonies voted to ratify the Constitution, each proposed amendments to remedy the omission. Over one hundred amendments were proposed. Some forty to fifty were eliminated as duplications. Seventeen were finally approved by the House of the First Congress; the Senate reduced the number to twelve, which were sent to the various legislatures for ratification. The final returns showed that ten had been ratified" (J. Reuben Clark, Jr. as quoted in Duane S. Crowther, *America: God's Chosen Land of Liberty*, p. 26).

[4] *Banner*, p. 31.

you that to me the Constitution of the United States of America is just as much from my Heavenly Father as the Ten Commandments."[5]

The Lord placed His approval on the Constitution in these words: "According to the laws and constitution of the people, which I have suffered to be established, and should be maintained for the rights and protection of all flesh, according to just and holy principles...have *I established the Constitution* [of the United States] *by the hands of wise men whom I raised up unto this very purpose...*" (Doctrine & Covenants 101:77-80; hereafter cited as D&C). He also said, "I, the Lord, justify you, and your brethren of my church, in befriending that law which is the constitutional law of the land" (D&C 98:6). And at the dedication of the Kirtland Temple, the Prophet Joseph prayed: "May those principles, which were so honorably and nobly defended, namely the Constitution of our land, by our fathers, be established forever" (D&C 109:54).

Concerning the Prophet Joseph Smith, he was one of the greatest patriots America has ever seen. He once said of himself, "I am the greatest advocate of the Constitution of the United States there is on earth."[6] His thoughts turned to Constitutional principles often, even at those times when he was allowed no such principles. While imprisoned in Liberty Jail the Prophet wrote: "The Constitution of the United States is a glorious standard; and is founded in the wisdom of God. It is a heavenly banner; it is to all those who are privileged with the sweets of liberty, like the cooling shades and refreshing waters of a great rock in a thirsty and weary land. It is like a great tree under whose branches men from every clime can be shielded from the burning rays of the sun."[7]

---

5 *CR*, April 1948, p. 182.
6 As quoted in Alma P. Burton, *Doctrines of the Prophets*, p. 43.
7 *TPJS*, p. 147.

In a time when faith and prayer are giving way to doubt and jarring, and when our sacred document the Constitution is not regarded as inspired from heaven, it would be wise to remember that "The Constitution of this government was written by men who accepted Jesus Christ as the Savior of mankind."[8] It was under such acceptance of the Lord that they dictated the Constitution by His inspiration. One incident during the Constitutional Convention exemplifies this fact. It is reported that Benjamin Franklin said to his brethren: "In the beginning...we had daily prayers in this room...Our prayers...were heard and they were generously answered.... I have lived a long time and the longer I live the more convincing proofs I see of this truth—that God governs in the affairs of men." Then boldly imprinting this theme on their minds he said: "If a sparrow cannot fall to the ground without His notice, is it possible that an empire can rise without His aid?"[9]

President Lorenzo Snow gave these stirring words: "We look upon George Washington, the father of our country, as an inspired instrument of the Almighty; we can see the all-inspiring Spirit operating upon him. And upon his co-workers in resisting oppression, and in establishing the thirteen colonies as a confederacy; and then again the workings of the same Spirit upon those men who established the Constitution of the United States."[10]

The Constitution has many hallmarks, but none greater than the fact that God inspired it!

---

8   *Discourses of the Prophet Joseph Smith*, p. 42.
9   As quoted in *The Teachings of Ezra Taft Benson*, p. 597.
10 *The Teachings of Lorenzo Snow*, p. 191.

Is the Constitution Perfect?

Brigham Young posed a provocative question when he asked: "The signers of the Declaration of Independence and the framers of the Constitution were inspired from on high to do that work. But was that which was given to them perfect, not admitting of any addition whatever?" President Young then answered his own question: "No; for if men know anything, they must know that the Almighty has never yet found a man in mortality that was capable, at the first intimation, at the first impulse, to receive anything in a state of entire perfection." This in part explains why the Constitution has received many amendments. The Founding Fathers "laid the foundation," but it was for "[later] generations to rear the superstructure upon it. It is a progressive—a gradual work."[11]

By way of explanation President John Taylor said: "[The Constitution], good as it was, was not a perfect instrument; it was one of those stepping stones to a future development in the progress of a man to the intelligence and light, the power and union that God alone can impart to the human family."[12] Even one of the signers, Benjamin Franklin, expressed the same sentiments when he said, "I agree to this Constitution *even with all its faults.*" He also added, "From such an [imperfect] assembly [as this Constitutional assembly] can a perfect production be expected? [Yet] It...astonishes me...to find this system approaching so near perfection as it does; and I think it will astonish our enemies."

Some people may surmise it contradictory to say in one instant that the Constitution was inspired by God, then at another moment say it is not perfect. But this is not hard to comprehend when we realize that even the Bible, which most of the Christian world regard as inspired, is not a perfect

---

[11]   *JD* 7:14.
[12]   *JD* 21:31

book, omitting any error. If it is a perfect book then why are there so many contradictions in the sacred volume? And why are so many books considered "lost" from the holy pages?[13] Despite all the weaknesses that abound in the Holy Bible, it is nonetheless an inspired record detailing God's dealings with His children. It was indeed inspired to be written and compiled, and, as such, has been a source of strength, guidance, and peace for countless millions who have turned to the divine book. The same is true with regard to our beloved Constitution.

Prelude to Restoration

Another great hallmark of the American Constitution is that its establishment prepared the way for the restoration of the Lord's Church. The restoration of the ancient order could only come about in an environment that applauded human dignity and religious freedom. And while it is a sad fact that the United States has upon its historic annals much stain concerning its dealings with the Lord's people, in no other nation could the restoration have taken place and succeeded in its divinely appointed mission. It could not have been established in a communistic society

---

13   Here is a list of the *lost books* as mentioned in the Old Testament: The book of the Covenant (Exo. 24:7); the book of the Wars of the Lord (Num. 21:14); the book of Jasher (Josh. 10:13; 2 Sam. 1:18); the book of the Manner of the Kingdom (1 Sam. 10:25); books containing 3000 proverbs, 1005 songs, and a treatise on natural history by Solomon (1 Kings 4:32, 33); the Acts of Solomon (1 Kings 11:14); the book of Gad the Seer (1 Chron 24:29); the book of Nathan the prophet (1 Chron. 24:29; 2 Chron. 9:29); the Prophecy of Ahijah, the Shilonite (2 Chron. 9:29); the Visions of Iddo the Seer (2 Chron. 9:29); the book of Shemaiah the prophet (2 Chron. 12:15); the story of the prophet Iddo (2 Chron. 13:22); the book of Jehu 2 Chron. 20:34). The *lost books* as mentioned in the New Testament are as follows: Another Epistle of Jude (Jude 3); another Epistle to the Ephesians (Eph. 3:3); another Epistle to the Laodiceans (Col. 9:16); another Epistle to the Corinthians (Cor. 5:9). (See *A Comprehensive History of the Church*, Vol. I, p. 249.)

where freedom was nothing more than a far-off dream; nor could it have succeeded in a country overrun by tyrants. Relating to this fact, President George Albert Smith commented:

> In no other nation under heaven could the Church have been organized and gone forward as we have in this nation. The founding of the United States was not an accident. The giving to us the Constitution was not an accident. Our Heavenly Father knew what would be needed, and so he paved the way to give us the Constitution. It came about under prayer, and he guided those who framed that wonderful document.[14]

And President Brigham Young said,

> It was the Lord who directed the discovery of this land to the nations of the old world, and its settlement, and the war of independence, and the final victory of the colonies, and the unprecedented prosperity of the American nation, up to the calling of Joseph the Prophet. The Lord has dictated the whole of this, for the bringing forth, and the establishing of his kingdom in the last days.[15]

The restoration, as long foreseen by prophets of old, commenced in 1820 when the lad Joseph Smith entered a grove of trees now made sacred by the event that transpired within its foliage. He entered with only a third grade education; he emerged as a prophet who beheld God and His Son. The official Church organization took place in upstate New York, April 6, 1830, just forty-one years from when the Constitution was first ratified.

---

[14] *TGAS*, p. 167.
[15] *JD* 11:17

3
A Tribute to
the American Flag

And the star-spangled Banner in triumph
shall wave O'er the land of the free
and the home of the brave!

—Francis Scott Key

For centuries, emperors, monarchs, and military leaders alike have displayed symbols that stood for their imperial or political orientation. Often the symbol has taken the form of a banner, or flag. Usually these banners headed armies and were posted on fortresses. When cities were overtaken, the victors' flags were hoisted for all to see.

Yet flags have not always represented the politics or governments of men, but often mans religious convictions as well. In the scriptures, for instance, a banner is often mentioned in the abstract. The Psalmist wrote of the Lord: "We will rejoice in thy salvation, and *in the name of our God we will set our banners*" (Psalms 20:5). David also praised, "*Thou hast given a banner to them that fear thee, that it may be displayed because of the truth*" (Psalms 60:4).

The Book of Mormon implies that a banner is a standard or ensign to a people (see 2 Nephi 29:4). Writing on this theme, Elder Bruce R. McConkie explained: "When Isaiah promised that the Lord would 'set up an ensign for the nations' and gather the dispersed of Israel, the ensign, the standard, *the divine flag around which all men should rally was to be the holy gospel.*"[1] In exponential terms, a flag represents a certain standard a people or nation possess, and when upheld becomes an ensign for all to see.

Captain Moroni's Title of Liberty

The Book of Mormon tells of one Captain Moroni who headed an army against an evil monarch named Amalickiah. Moroni, stirring his men to conviction, "rent his coat; and...took a piece thereof, and wrote upon it— *In memory of our God, our religion, and freedom, and our peace, our wives, and our children*—and he fastened it upon the end of a pole." After doing so, "he went forth among the people, waving the rent part of his garment in the air, *that all might see* the writing which he had written upon the rent part, and crying with a loud voice, saying: Behold, whosoever will maintain the title [flag] in the land, let them come forth in the strength of the Lord, and enter into a covenant that they will maintain their rights, and their religion, that the Lord God may bless them" (Alma 46:12, 19-20). Moroni's makeshift flag became a standard to his people, an ensign to the Nephites. It was their *Title of Liberty.* Yet it wasn't Captain Moroni's worn coat that stirred his people to conviction; it was what it represented.

---

1   *The Millennial Messiah: The Second Coming of the Son of Man*, pp. 106-107; hereafter cited as *The Millennial Messiah.* President John Taylor commented on this same passage from Isaiah, saying: "Now, a standard, or ensign, is a nation's colours [sic], flag, or rallying point; it is one of those appendages to a kingdom that is always respected by its inhabitants" (*The Government of God*, pp. 93-94).

The Stars and Stripes

Perhaps the greatest of all flags ever fabricated by the hand of man is the national flag of the United States of America. Like Moroni's Title of Liberty, the real significance behind the Stars and Stripes lies not necessarily in its fabrication (though its very creation is filled with symbolism and inspiring overtones), but in its representation.[2] A brief history is given here concerning the flag's evolution from humble beginnings to vibrant life. The *Encyclopedia Americana* explains:

> Within the colonies local flags gradually developed. In 18th-century New England, for example, troops sent to fight native people or the French displayed colors devised by themselves. At first most of these were similar to European models, but as a distinctive American culture developed, designs began to show characteristic local emblems, such as the beaver or the pine.
>
> At the start of the American Revolution each military unit selected its own flag: at sea the profusion of American flags was so great that foreign powers were bewildered. Gen. George Washington and others often expressed the need for standardization, but more pressing matters prevented any action from being taken on military standards. In the case for the national flag for use at sea, however, it was evident that a single flag had to be adopted so that foreign powers would not regard American ships as mere privateers.

---

[2] "So far as I am concerned," said Elder Mark E. Peterson, "the flag of the United States is the flag of Almighty God. Old Glory to me stands for everything that the gospel of Christ stands for, because Old Glory was raised up because there was to be a restoration of the gospel. I cannot separate my flag and my religion. I would fight for my flag as I would fight for my religion" (*BYU Speeches of the Year*, February 20, 1968, p. 10).

In January 1776 Washington, proclaiming the organization of
the Continental army, raised the Continental Colors. This red-
and-white-striped flag with the British Union Jack as its canton
was the unofficial national flag until the Continental Congress
adopted the 13-star, 13-stripe U.S. national flag on June 14, 1777.[3]

The Congressional Journal for the day the flag was adopted mentions
only formal proceedings. No mention of the discussions that attended
them is given. As if by fate, however, one entry records the historic words,

> RESOLVED: that the flag of the United States be made of thir-
> teen stripes, alternate red and white; that the union be thirteen
> stars, white in a blue field, representing a new constellation.

Since no official blueprint for the flag's image was listed, but only a
brief sketch, the upstart nation saw numerous flags fashioned in various
ways. "The stars might be arranged in a circle, in rows, or with 12 stars
encircling a 13th, and the stars had from 4 to 8 points. The stripes, too,
varied: sometimes they were vertical, and, despite the official resolution,
flags frequently had blue stripes as well as red and white ones."[4] The flag
that gained most appeal, however, was one sewn by Betsy Ross, who placed
the stars in a circular position set against a blue field.[5] By 1794 Betsy
Ross' flag was replaced by a flag that contained two new stars (representing
the addition of Vermont and Kentucky to the Union), including two
additional stripes. This was the official flag of the United States from 1795
to 1818.

---

[3] *Encyclopedia Americana*, p. 351.

[4] Ibid. p. 352.

[5] William J. Canby, a grandson of Betsy Ross, claimed that his grandmother sewed
the first United States flag. Although Ross *was* a flag-maker there is no valid proof
that substantiates Canby's claim, as it is based entirely on oral family tradition.

The evolution of the American flag was not over yet, but was to experience even more change. If a stripe were added to the flag every time a state joined the Union, the obvious thing would happen: the flag would develop to enormous proportions. To prevent this from happening, Peter Wendover, a representative from New York, proposed to Congress that an additional star be added to the flag representing the addition of the new state, but proposed the stripes remain thirteen in number. Following Wendover's suggestion, President Monroe advised that a new star be added to the blue field on the succeeding July 4th after a state was admitted to the Union. The stripes have since remained thirteen in number, representing the original colonies.

The Star Spangled Banner

It would be ironic to discuss the American flag without mentioning something of the country's national anthem—that poetic song that was inspired by the Stars and Stripes. *The Star Spangled Banner* is sung at the opening sessions of sporting events; it is sung in religious gatherings and convocations across the nation, and in the hearts and minds of patriots throughout the country. But the story of its inspiring creation is little known, and is worth retelling here. In doing so we must go back to the year 1812.

> At the start of the War of 1812, Maj. George Armistead, the commander of Fort McHenry, which guarded the entrance to Baltimore harbor, ordered an American flag "so large that the British will have no difficulty in seeing it from a distance."
>
> Commissioned to produce the special banner was Mary Pickersgill, who sewed flags professionally in her Baltimore home. The project was so large—the flag was originally 30 feet wide and 42 feet long—that she had to use space nearby Clagett's brewery

to lay out the English wool bunting. Pickersgill's 13-year-old daughter, Caroline Purdy, helped with the flag, which was completed in August 1813 and cost $405.90.[6]

It was through pen and inspiration that the national anthem came to life. A young attorney by the name of Francis Scott Key played the author. Elder Vaughn J. Featherstone explained Key's dramatic role in writing *The Star Spangled Banner,* while also explaining a common misconception. Elder Featherstone writes:

> A common misconception is that Francis Scott Key composed the anthem as a prisoner of war of the British Fleet that attacked Fort McHenry at Baltimore. But in truth, he was not a prisoner of war. Early in September 1814, the British Fleet floated in the Chesapeake Bay off Baltimore after British naval and land forces had taken Washington, burned government facilities, and taken prisoner Dr. William Beanes. Key, an influential Washington attorney, was persuaded by friends of Dr. Beanes to negotiate for his release. He went to Baltimore and with Col. J. S. Skinner, government agent for the exchange of prisoners, went in a sloop to meet the fleet. British Admiral Sir George Cockburn courteously received them, and the release of Dr. Beanes was agreed upon. However, because the proposed attack on Baltimore had been discussed in the presence of the Americans, Key, Col. Skinner, and Dr. Beanes were returned to the sloop and kept under guard behind the British lines until after the attack.[7]

---

[6] "Inspiration: How U.S. Anthem Was Born," *The Salt Lake Tribune,* December 6, 1998, A-1.

[7] *More Purity Give Me,* pp. 73-74.

It was the night of September 13-14 that the battle took place. Key anxiously stayed on deck and watched the ensuing bombardment of Fort McHenry. When morning came—"the dawns early light"—the young attorney saw that "the flag was still there" amidst debris and destruction. The sight so inspired him that he retrieved a letter from his pocket and began to write. The words flowed with inspiration. When Key finished his composition the United States of America had its national anthem. Though it wasn't until 1916 that President Woodrow Wilson "issued an executive order designating it the official anthem. Congress confirmed [the] act in 1931."[8]

A Personal Tribute

I am not as great a man as was Moroni, but like Moroni I feel a great love for the Lord. And like Moroni, I possess a great admiration for my country. I cherish the freedoms that are mine, and I have great respect for the honored symbols of my nation. As stated in the preface of this work, I feel great awe whenever I see the Stars and Stripes wave its freedom flying colors in the breeze. I believe the National Flag of the United States of America to be a sacred emblem. I feel reverent awe whenever I ponder its symbolism and significance. I also believe, as did Brigham Young, Ezra Taft Benson, and other individuals, that the flag of the United States will be flying over the covenant people of the Lord when He comes again. These sentiments, as well as the reverence I feel for the flag of my country, inspired within me a short poem which I have titled, like unto Moroni, *My Title of Liberty*:

8   "Inspiration: How U.S. National Anthem Was Born," *The Salt Lake Tribune*, December 6, 1998, A-4.

My Title of Liberty

My Title of Liberty, e'er she waves
In heaven's blue sky, against the sun's burning rays.
Her colors majestic, so triumphant and bright,
Sends warmth to my soul—for freedom I will fight!

America is precious, a jewel from above.
And by God's omnipotent grace and His infinite love
I know *My Title of Liberty* will in that day stand,
When the Lord comes to redeem this sacred land;

Those patriot colors will yet fly in the breeze,
And all men will know as they fall upon their knees,
That the King has come to rule and reign,
More Terrible and Holy than every other name.

Unto America is where Zion will stand,
In earth's corner, 'twas Lehi's Promised Land;
Where right is right, and men are free,
Forever will be established *My Title of Liberty*!

Part II:
PERSPECTIVES ON AMERICA'S PRESENT

The problems of the world cannot possibly
be solved by the skeptics or cynics
whose horizons are limited
by the obvious realities.

—Spencer W. Kimball

4
Patriots & Defenders of Liberty

Where the Spirit of the Lord is, there is liberty.

—2 Corinthians 3:17

Where liberty dwells, there is my country.

—John Milton

The Prophet Joseph Smith said, "We want to live in peace with all men; and equal rights is all we ask."[1] It seems ironic that the many petitions the Prophet sent before Congress for redress of the wrongs heaped upon the Church were never granted. He and the saints were never shown the smallest amount of "equal rights" from the government that proposed them. After the martyrdom the saints, lead by Brigham Young, went west to find their goodly land of promise whereby they could worship the Lord unmolested by a hypocritical government. In doing so they left the United

---

[1]   *HC* 2:122.

States and entered Mexican territory. It wasn't until 1896 that Utah was annexed by the United States and became the forty-eighth state of the Union. Thankfully today things are much better between the Church and the nation. The government, for the most part, respects the Church, although it does not understand it. Perhaps when the latter-day saints stand fast to defend the Constitution will the government then understand, at least to a greater degree, The Church of Jesus Christ of Latter-day Saints.

The Constitution itself is not a trite work of political jargon, but rather a hallowed decree confirming our God-given, unalienable rights. The latter-day saints believe this wholeheartedly, though not all people believe this. Countless attacks are made against the American Constitution that a deadly ruin will result if the tides do not change course. Latter-day saints are familiar with the alleged prophecy by Joseph Smith wherein he noted the almost complete destruction of the Constitution. "Even this nation," said the Prophet, " will be on the very verge of crumbling to pieces and tumbling to the ground, and…the Constitution…upon the brink of ruin."[2] Despite the knowing prophecies, however, it does not exclude us from doing all in our power to try and preserve the integrity of that sacred document and the heritage of our noble land. In fact, the Prophet said: "If the Constitution is to be saved at all, it will be by the latter-day saints."[3] True patriots and defenders of liberty are vastly needed today! We invite people of all faiths to join the battle ranks with us in defending the Constitution. The Poet Wordsworth beckoned in verse:

Come ye—whate'er your creed—O waken all,
Whate'er your temper, at your Country's call.

---

[2]   *Discourses of the Prophet Joseph Smith*, p. 304.
[3]   Ibid.

Freedom—the Most Prized Possession

To be victorious against the attacks aimed at our freedom we must first realize who the enemy is, what his tactics are, and how best to combat them. We must also realize that the battle for freedom has been fought since the dawn of time. The enemy is the adversary of all righteousness, the father of lies, the prince of darkness, the author of evil and captivity. In the Grand Council of heaven before the earth's foundations were laid, it was Lucifer, "son of the morning," who sought to destroy the free agency of the sons and daughters of God. In proposing His plan of salvation and explaining our need for a Redeemer, our Heavenly Father asked, "Whom shall I send?" Then "one answered like unto the Son of Man," even Jehovah, saying, "Here am I, send me" (Abraham 3:27), and humbly adding, "Father, thy will be done, and the glory be thine forever" (Moses 4:2). But scheming Lucifer, once an angel of light, said, "Behold, here am I, send me, and I will redeem all mankind, that not one soul shall be lost, and surely I will do it; wherefore give me thine honor" (Moses 4:1). Heavenly Father made His decision: "I will send the first." The Apostle John recorded in his apocalypse what happened next:

> And there was war in heaven: Michael and his angels fought against the dragon; and the dragon fought and his angels, and prevailed not; neither was there place found any more in heaven. And the great dragon was cast out, that old serpent, called the Devil, and Satan. Which deceiveth the whole world: he was cast into the earth, and his angels were cast out with him (Revelation 12:7-9).

The Lord explains that warfare took place "because that Satan rebelled against me, and sought to destroy the agency of man, which I the Lord God, had given him, and also, that I should give unto him mine own power; by the power of mine Only Begotten, [therefore] I caused that he should be cast out" (Moses 4:3).

With the prominence he held as an "angel of light" Lucifer gain a following of one-third of heaven's population. Each were denied a mortal experience, yet each were "cast into the earth...with him [Lucifer]" (Revelation 12:9). As an evil spirit on earth Lucifer is known as Satan, "the devil, the father of all lies, to deceive and to blind men, and to lead them captive at his will" (Moses 4:4). Such is the ambition of the Adversary and his minions—to make all men miserable like unto themselves.

Alfred Lord Tennyson penned immortal words when he wrote: "Of old sat freedom on the heights." When Michael and his angels fought against the dragon it was in defense of freedom—our agency. Each of us played crucial roles during the pre-mortal councils; each of us exercised our agency and either chose to follow the Father's plan of salvation, whereby our agency would be preserved, or to follow Lucifer's diabolical imitation. Our mortal bodies attest that we chose the Father's plan, that we accepted Jehovah as our promised Savior, that we wanted to be free.[4] However, "The war that began in heaven is not yet over," said President Ezra Taft Benson. "The conflict continues on the battlefield of mortality." Although freedom's issues triumphed during the war in heaven, freedom's cause has rarely been won on earth. "Look back in retrospect on almost six thousand years of human history!" President Benson continues. "Freedom's moments have been infrequent and exceptional." Then as a stirring reminder President Benson said: *"Freedom as we know it has been experienced by perhaps less than one percent of the human family."*[5]

We live in a remarkable time in the history of the earth. Never has mankind been the beneficiary of so much. We are the recipients of countless blessings, both temporal and otherwise. We enjoy the kind of freedom that no other time period or people have ever enjoyed. We live in a world

---

4   Richard L. Evans said that "Freedom is a God-given, inalienable right and is essential to the soul's salvation in the highest sense. And every man must be protected in his right to choose as to certain essentials" (*Richard Evans' Quote Book*, p. 90, hereafter cited as *Evans*).

5   *Banner*, pp. 3-4; emphasis added.

struggling for democracy and yet we, as American citizens, are favored with the sweets of liberty—a beacon to all! It cannot be overstated: we are blessed with so much freedom! We have freedom of religion, freedom of speech, freedom of the press; we have the right to bear arms, the right to peaceably assemble, the right to travel, to work, to attend schools of higher learning. We are free to take simple walks at sunset, we are free to hunt, to fish, and to vote. Because we are a republic that enjoys so much freedom it is hard for us to imagine ever being without it. Yet we must come to the clear realization that there are infringements being made now that threaten many of the freedoms we take for granted. President Spencer W. Kimball said:

> ...a lot of us take our civil rights for granted. We were born in a free country. We think freedom could never end. But it could. It is ending today in many countries. *We could lose it too.*[6]

Most of the ways in which are freedoms can be taken from us are not thought of, or at most not believed. But excess government control, creeping socialism, the bondage of debt, spiritual apathy, and sin are all ways that can and do erode dimensions of our freedom, either temporally or spiritually. As President Benson said, the battle that begun in heaven is not yet over, and just because the Cold War has ended doesn't mean the battle doesn't still rage. If we care enough about our freedom than it only seems right that we would do the things that would help protect our freedom. President Kimball taught: "The only way we can keep freedom is to work at it. Not some of us. All of us. Not some of the time, but all of the time."[7]

The remainder of this chapter confronts some of the issues contending against freedom and patriotism today. The first discussion concerns threats to our spiritual freedom.

---

6   *TSWK*, p. 405; emphasis added.
7   Ibid.

The Bondage of Sin

While the United States enjoys the abundant fruits of a temporal freedom, she is deficient and malnourished in spiritual freedom. Where spiritual freedom is lacking, the bondage of sin abounds. This is where Jesus' calling as Savior and Redeemer has personal meaning.

In proclaiming His gospel to the Jews, the Savior said, "ye shall know the truth, and the truth shall make you free" (John 8:32). Exactly what truth was He referring to? What truth could make the Jews—and us—free? And what exactly would we be free from? Let's use the Jews as an example to answer these questions.

First of all, we must understand that the Jews to whom Christ came were steeped in Mosaic tradition. They clung fanatically to the precepts taught by the great prophet Moses. Yet their zeal to the law outweighed their devotion to the Lawgiver, Jehovah. Thus when Christ came among the Jews and proclaimed Himself to be the Great I AM, and teaching higher laws than Sinai, the Jews scoffed Him, mocked Him, and crucified Him. To the uncomprehending and unbelieving He was known only as Jesus of Nazareth, a carpenter's son, a blasphemer worthy of death. But to the receptive and believing He was more than a man. Concerning the overzealous Jews and their intimations, author Joseph Fielding McConkie analyzed the following:

> It was not the law given on Sinai that governed the people to whom Christ and his disciples preached but the traditions that like wild vines had overgrown it. "The Law—not the Law in its simplicity but the Law modified, transformed, distorted by tradition—the Law robbed of its essential significance by the blind zeal which professed to defend it—became the centre of an abject servility. It came to be regarded as the only means of intercourse with God, *and almost as the substitute for God.* Immeasurable evils ensued. Piety dwindled into legalism. Salvation was identified

with outward conformity." Pharisaism reigned supreme. *So important did study of religious traditions become that it would yet be said by one of the famed rabbis that God himself spent three hours a day studying the Torah.*[8]

In their zealous and sinful fanaticism the Jews failed to comprehend the true mission of the Mortal Messiah. When Christ came among them they had no perception of His divine authority. Though the Jews looked forward to a messiah, the messiah to whom they looked was not a babe born in a stable in the obscure town of Bethlehem. Rather, the Jews anticipated their messiah to be a great warrior, one that would deliver the Jewish nation from the yoke of Roman bondage. The Jews failed to recognize that all the prophecies of the Old Testament foretold the Messiah to be a comely looking man (see Isaiah 53:2; also see Mosiah 14:2), a man born of woman. Christ came to free not only the Jews but the whole world, not from the yoke of government bondage but from the bondage of sin. He was a man, yes—but He was also so much more than a man!

Jesus Christ, the Old Testament's Jehovah, came the first time as the humble babe of Bethlehem for whom the star shone. He came as the Great Teacher and Exemplar of eternal truth. He was the very embodiment of truth! He came not as a political warrior but as a Warrior for our sins and as our Champion over death. Through Christ's atonement the good news is that we have been set free from Adam's transgression; we are not accountable for other peoples' sin (see Article of Faith 3). We are made free from an everlasting physical death; our spirit and body will reunite, becoming an immortal, tangible body. And we can be set free from individual sin; we can be washed in Christ's tender forgiveness, becoming clean without spot or blemish. The first two objectives have freely been given to us as *gifts* of the atonement. There was no effort on our part to obtain them. This last objective, however, becoming clean from sin, is

---

8   *Here We Stand,* pp. 13-14; emphasis added.

conditioned upon our acceptance of Christ and our repentance unto Him. Only as we begin to comprehend His love for us will we begin to understand more fully just what His atonement can mean to us. President Ezra Taft Benson simplified the message of the Messiah by saying:

> The Lord works from the inside out. The world works from the outside in. The world would take people out of the slums. Christ takes the slums out of people, who then take themselves out of the slums. The world would mold men by changing their environment. Christ changes men, who then change their environment. The world would shape human behavior, but Christ can change human nature.... Yes, Christ changes men, and changed men can change the world.[9]

If we are not careful, if we do not repent quickly and often, then we, like the Jews of Jesus' time, can become desensitized to the Spirit of Truth and fail to recognize its quiet yet divine whisperings. If we do exercise faith unto repentance, however, the Savior can and will change us. And as a prophet of God has testified, changed people "can change the world" around them. Ultimately we can do much more good in society if we are spiritually set free through Christ's atonement than we could by being a bondservant to sin. Faith in Christ adds character to an individual, and ultimately it is personal character that adds to the collective character of society.

Government Oppression

Aside from sin one of the adversary's most successful attempts at hindering human freedom is through molested and corrupt government. One

---

[9]   *TETB*, p. 79.

example of a government gone cockeyed is observed through the words of the Marquis de Custine. While visiting Russia in the nineteenth century, the Marquis wrote:

> One needs to have lived in that solitude without tranquility, that prison without leisure that is called Russia, to appreciate all the freedom enjoyed in other European countries, no matter what form of government they have chosen.... It is always good to know that there exists a society in which no happiness is possible, because, by reason of his nature, man cannot be happy unless he is free.[10]

Government oppression like the Marquis observed in Russia may seem far from reality here in America. Nevertheless, "we live in a time of great anxiety—a time when the basic concepts and values of a free society, which we cherish, are being seriously challenged...from dangerous ideologies and practices here at home."[11] Some of these dangerous ideologies stem from many roots, though many persons are ambivalent to them. Some of the threats against freedom in America are from incorrect government policy, the conspirator welfare state, and from the welfare state-of-mind. Elder Ezra Taft Benson wisely observed:

> It is true that outwardly everything seems prosperous. More people are working at higher wages and enjoying a better standard of living than ever before in the history of our country. More of our people are enjoying travel, cultural and educational opportunities than at any time in our history. New churches are being erected at a rapid rate and an increasing number of people are church-affiliated. Our nation is at peace.

---

10   As quoted in *Foreign Affairs*, Jan/Feb 1997, p. 49.
11   *So Shall Ye Reap*, p. 195.

All these things should give a feeling of stability, inner assurance, and a sense of satisfaction, but they do not seem to do so. Discontent among our people, nation-wide, seems to be high. We view with alarm the ever rising level of public and private debt and the threat of inflation. We note with fear the increase in crime, juvenile delinquency, alcoholism, drug addiction, and sex offences.

We pay lip service to the principles embodied in the Declaration of Independence and the Constitution without realizing what they are and the danger of ignoring them. We demand more and more of government, so "Government grows larger all the while, making the stampede-away from personal responsibility which occurs at all levels of life." We passively contribute to the spirit and demoralizing philosophy of "something for nothing."[12]

Elder Benson's words are as true today as when he first spoke them. They are intricate with careful and prophetic insight and coated with caution. Elder Benson continues his analysis by saying:

Even among free nations we see the encroachment of government upon the lives of the citizenry by excessive taxation and regulation, all done under the guise that the people would not willfully or charitably distribute their wealth, so the government must take it from them. We further observe promises by the state of security, whereby men are taken care of from the womb to the tomb rather than earning this security by the "sweat of their brow;" deception in high places, with the justification that "the end justifies the means;" atheism; agnosticism; immorality; and dishonesty. The attendant results of such sin and usurpation of power are a general

---

12   Ibid. "If a nation values anything more than freedom it will lose its freedom; and the irony of it is that if it is comfort or money that if values more, it will lose that too" (William Somerest Maugham, as quoted in *Evans'*, p. 90).

distrust of government officials; an insatiable, covetous spirit for more and more material wants; personal debt to satisfy this craving; and the disintegration of the family unit.[13]

It appears from Elder Benson's analysis that government oppression and the public's insatiable appetite to gratify the flesh is closely intertwined.[14] It is easy for a government to become a depressor of people when the people have depressed themselves into false ideologies. President David O. McKay said: "The state should have no power but that which the people give it; and when the state becomes a director, a controller of the individual, it becomes despotism; and human nature has fought that since man was created; and man will continue to fight that false ideal."[15] If we should continue to fight this false ideal then we must awake to the "obvious realities" about us.

There are many ways in which our freedoms can be stripped from us, either temporally or spiritually, and government oppression is only one. There are also many ways to safeguard our freedoms. Let us here discuss some of the hindrances we face in today's crucial time, as well as our obligations to defend our freedom.

---

13 *This Nation Shall Endure*, p. 8. "Freedom cannot live after the family as we know it is dead. Freedom cannot out-live morality" (Thomas Andersen, as quoted in *Evans'*, p. 87).

14 "If men be good," said William Penn, "government cannot be bad" (as quoted in *Evans'*, p. 92).

15 *Gospel Ideals*, p. 307. "I believe there are more instances of the abridgment of the freedom of the people," said James Madison, "by gradual and silent encroachments of those in power, than by violent and sudden usurpation." This danger, warned Madison, "ought to be wisely guarded against" (As quoted in W. Cleon Skousen, *The Five Thousand Year Leap*, p. 166). The Founding Fathers knew the threat of government and the oppression it would bring if not harnessed. "Government is not reason," said George Washington, "it is not eloquence—it is force! Like fire it is a dangerous servant and a fearful master" (Ibid., p. 165).

Following Sound Counsel

In being true patriots and defenders of liberty we must take the precaution to not follow unknown or uninspired voices, especially when those voices contradict or attack the prophetic voice. One of the Lord's duly authorized servants has given this wise counsel to Church members:

> There are many among us now who have not been regularly ordained by the heads of the Church who tell of impending political chaos, the end of the world—something of the "sky is falling, chicken licken'" of the fables. They are misleading members to gather to colonies or to cults. Those deceivers say that the Brethren do not know what is going on in the world or that the Brethren approve of their teaching but do not wish to speak of it over the pulpit. *Neither is true.* The Brethren, by virtue of travelling constantly everywhere on earth, certainly know what is going on, and by virtue of prophetic insight are able to read the signs of the times…. Come away from any others. *Follow your leaders who have been duly ordained and have been publicly sustained, and you will not be lead astray.*[16]

Often we hear of people who have fled their job and home, and in some instances family, to seek isolation in a mountainous region or a desert shack. Many join militia movements, this because they become over-anxious about government and anticipate government ruin. Even some Church members have become involved with such wayward anticipation. Some become fanatical, while others become radical. Still others fall by the wayside and become apathetic to the serious conflicts raging

---

[16]   Boyd K. Packer, as quoted in Hoyt W. Brewster, *Behold, I Come Quickly*, pp. 9-10; emphasis added.

about them. Yet this would never be the case if all members followed the sound counsel and patriot examples of our prophetic Church leaders. "If you want to walk in the light, " said President Harold B. Lee, "keep your eyes on the president [of the Church]." In doing so, as Elder Packer said, you "will not be lead astray."

Fanatical Extremists

There are many people and organizations today that, however good their intentions may be, teach unsound doctrines related to the American theme. Concerning one of them, world revered novelist and best-selling author, James A. Michener analyzed:

> A disturbing development is the proliferation, especially in the West and the South, of so-called militia units. These are paramilitary groups of men and women with guns and uniforms who train like soldiers in the countryside, practicing against the day when they may have to defend themselves against the tyranny of the government.... The members of the militias are *intensely patriotic*, and they yearn to return to the good old days of family solidants. They *despise our present government*, especially if it happens to be in Democratic hands; they are committed both to their beliefs that government is secretly plotting to deprive them of their freedoms and to their intrigues against the government. While they are not openly racist, they are preponderantly white Anglo-Saxons and their ranks provide a haven for those who fear the ultimate domination of the races of color, whether the imagined enemy happens to be black, brown or yellow.

Passionately they believe they have been organized to save the nation from revolution and expect to be called to arms in the foreseeable future…a goodly number of their rabid members claim to be born-again right-wing Christians.[17]

While the *average* citizen may not hear too much about the activities or practices of militia movements, unless of course they make news headlines of some sort, Michener's analysis was not in vain. Many groups as that mentioned above are active in the pursuit of what they tern "ideal patriotism," though in reality their ideal is more fanatical than anything else. Those who associate with such groups believe they are doing justice to our nation, when in reality they are doing nothing more than being a menace. The words of Joseph F. Smith are blunt and to the point:

> One of the greatest menaces to our country is that combination of men into irresponsible, reckless mobs, wild with prejudice, hatred and fanaticism, led by men of ambition, or passion, or hatred. There is no other thing in the world that I can conceive of being so absolutely obnoxious to God and good men as a combination of men and women filled with the spirit of mobocracy. Men combining together [in this manner] is one of the most infamous perils and menaces to the people of our country today. *I do not care who they are, or what name they go by. They are a menace to the peace of this world.*[18]

---

[17] *This Noble Land*, pp. 180-182; emphasis added. Neither Michener or this author is saying that all militia units are bad. Some are quite honorable of themselves. It is important, however, that we possess the spirit of discernment that we might know the good from the bad.

[18] *Gospel Doctrine*, pp. 414-15, emphasis added; hereafter cited as *GD*.

On the topic of fanaticism, Elder Bruce R. McConkie has written:

> Fanaticism is the devil's substitute for and perversion of true zeal. It is exhibited in wildly extravagant and overzealous views and acts. It is based on either an unreasoning devotion to a cause...or...an overemphasis of some particular doctrine or practice, an emphasis which twists the truth as a whole out of perspective.... *Stable and sound persons are never fanatics; they do not ride gospel hobbies.*[19]

There is logic and sound counsel in what Elder McConkie has written. Fanaticism, even when related to an otherwise virtuous teaching, is detrimental to any person's spiritual growth and can corrupt rational thinking. We can be patriotic, and indeed should be, without being "patriomanic."[20]

Radical Extremists

Not only does society struggle against the rampant siege of fanatical patriot groups but it also struggles against the onslaught of radical rights activists who promote new ideological advancements which attack the staple symbols of our country, one being the hideous act of flag burning. Flag burning was once upon a time condemned by our courts of law, but now has been turned into a "free speech" issue rather than the unjustified and treasonous crime that it is. One newspaper article on this subject explained: "The U.S. Supreme court in 1989 struck down flag protection in 48 states and the District of Columbia by ruling that those laws

---

19 *Mormon Doctrine*, p. 275; emphasis added.
20 Elder Boyd K. Packer said, patriotism "when pressed to the extreme, like other virtues will presently become a vice" (*Let Not Your Heart Be Troubled*, p. 67).

infringe on the constitutional guarantees of free speech."[21] *Speech* and *acts*, however, are two different things and there is no provision in the First Amendment that guarantees the right of individuals to act in this manner. As Elder Boyd K. Packer said, "Speech is made up of spoken or printed words. *Words are words are words. Acts are acts are acts.*"[22] The liberal agenda refuses to acknowledge this fact.

In vehement declaration, Elder Packer said: "The willful destruction of the flag that belongs to each of us is the act of an extremist. A court decision legalizing the destruction of it to protect the rights of one protestor is equally extreme."[23] And I might add—traitorous!

Though there are current efforts being made to restore legal protection to the flag, such efforts are not an end to the conflict. Until flag burning is viewed in its proper light—as an irreverent crime against the nation rather than a free speech issue—the problem will remain. But alas, let the efforts continue to be made! One day perhaps the flag will again be protected. "Restoring legal protection to the American flag would not infringe on free speech," said Senator Orrin Hatch. "Nor would restoring legal protection to the American flag place us on a slippery slope to limit other freedoms."[24] If Congress initiated more reverence toward the national flag, perhaps it would encourage a deeper morale in the general public; perhaps we would all think differently, more kindly, toward the flag. It would at least be a step in the right direction.

Thus while we prize our freedom we must neglect our loyalty. These words, again from Elder Packer, are the core of the matter: "Freedom [cannot] long survive in a society where the rights of the individual are

---

[21] "Hatch Again Pushes Amendment To Prohibit Burning of the Flag," *The Salt Lake Tribune,* February 5, 1998, A-1; hereafter cited as "Hatch."

[22] *Let Not Your Heart Be Troubled,* p. 67.

[23] Ibid.

[24] "Hatch."

fanatically promoted regardless of what happens to society itself."[25] He also said:

> The rights of the individual—the ideal, the virtue—when pressed to the extreme, like other virtues will presently become a vice. Unless they insure some balance, activists, lawyers, legislators, judges, and courts who think they are protecting individual freedom are in fact fabricating a new and sinister kind of dictatorship.[26]

The Problem with Apathy

Beside the danger that arises from fanatical and radical extremist groups, the American populace faces the gross problem of apathy. Perhaps apathy is the worst of all our problems. Apathetic people suggest that "such and such" could never happen in America or to them. They have the mistaken notion that "all is well," when in reality the truth is just the contrary. They go about their everyday lives, "eating and drinking, marrying and giving in marriage" (See JS-M 1:42), "ever learning, and never able to come to the knowledge of the truth" (2 Timothy 3:7). Apathy is when a person or persons are unaware and/or unconcerned of the problems about them. The scriptures teach, however, that "men should be anxiously engaged in a good cause, and do many things of their own free will" (D&C 58:27; see verses 26-28). Surely this principle condemns apathy. We need to be active, aware, and concerned citizens. But again we do not need to go to any extremes. There is a healthy, moderate balance to be obtained if we are to be true patriots and defenders of liberty. The example of our prophetic leaders should be our yardstick.

---

25   *Let Not Your Heart Be Troubled*, p. 67.
26   Ibid.

Though the battle is real, the victor's are few. While society favors apathy, the "few" strive for holy ground, safe havens and sure harbors, all the while becoming true patriots and defenders of liberty, ready to defend and take the Constitution to Zion and uphold its banners for all the world to see.

A Rejuvenation of the Principles of Patriotism

"Patriotism is something we feel as well as something we understand and know," said Elder Vaughn J. Featherstone. "It isn't always easy to describe."[27] We probably have all felt at one time or another the feelings of patriotism. Perhaps you have felt such stirrings when singing the national anthem or another patriotic song. Maybe you've felt patriotic while watching fireworks on the Fourth of July, or maybe while hearing a noble political campaign speech. Or perhaps you've felt patriotic, like me, when seeing the Stars and Stripes catch a breeze in the backdrop of a blue sky. Still, maybe patriotic feelings arise while working in a garden, or picnicking with family and friends, or while barbecuing in the cool of a summer's eve. These feelings, whenever we have them, are noble feelings. Most likely they bring to our minds the sacrifices our ancestors have made in order for us to enjoy the bounteous blessings of freedom we have today. Patriotic feelings make us proud of being American; they make us want to be good citizens; they make us want to serve our country in whatever capacity we can. Patriotic feelings may even have a calming influence, an inner pride for being American, which prompts feelings of gratitude to be living in a free society.

As important as patriotic feelings are, however, "patriotism is more than flag-waving and fireworks. It is how we respond to the public issues"[28] of the day. It is how we treat the law. It is how we treat our neighbors. It is what

---

[27] *More Purity Give Me*, p. 66.
[28] *So Shall Ye Reap*, p. 209.

we do for the country just as much as it is how we feel about the country. In very fact, if we truly are patriotic we will exemplify our patriotism by fulfilling our civic duty. Such duty has many facets. For example, it can be participating in PTA and other aspects of our children's education, or helping a political candidate advertise his platform; it can be giving time to a homeless shelter or other organizations; it can be participating in crime-watch programs, or campaigning against pornography. There are numerous ways we can give to our country, and each person has something significant to offer.

In his day President David O. McKay said: "Next to being one in worshipping God, there is nothing in this world upon which this Church should be more unified than in upholding and defending the Constitution of the United States."[29] The question is, *How can we best unite in defending the Constitution?* Elder Boyd K. Packer has given us the answer. "Let me tell you," he said. "Just go home and be decent, Sunday-go-to-meeting people. Teach your children decency and honor, cooperation and tolerance, citizenship and patriotism. Teach them to be good. Teach them to have a clear conscience."[30]

Notice where we're supposed to do the teaching? As with any teaching of lasting value it begins in the home, setting examples of "decency and honor" for our children to pattern after. "From homes such as these," said Elder Melvin J. Ballard, "have come the men and women who have made America great, the men who have furnished the sinew and leadership of the Church."[31] Elder Vaughn J. Featherstone taught the same principle. "A patriot's duty is continuous," he writes. "It starts in the home in family home evening by teaching precious children about their great land. The heroes of the parents generally become the heroes of the children. Every home in America ought to be burning with the flames of freedom represented in

---

30   *Let Not Your Heart Be Troubled*, p. 67.

31   *Sermons and Missionary Services of Melvin J. Ballard*, p. 21.

this country."[32] And the Prophet Joseph Smith taught that we should establish "*Our homes*, gardens, orchards, farms, streets, bridges, mills, public halls, magnificent Temple[s], and other public improvements…*as a monument to our patriotism.*"[33]

The counsel we have been given from our Church leaders becomes all the more poignant when we realize our children will not learn love and respect for country from society, even though schools do have the responsibility to help teach "patriotism and loyalty to the government and society."[34] We live in secular times, where good and evil are considered irrelevant. The schools of today will not teach patriotic values anymore than they will teach the time-adage Judeo-Christian values.

Though patriotism has many facets, there seems to be nothing flamboyant about it: the best way an individual can show patriotism to his country is by living the simple but good life of an honest, law-abiding citizen. President Joseph F. Smith iterated that "Patriotism should be sought for and will be found in right living."[35] We do not need to be an extremist, either right- or leftwing, but we also cannot afford to be apathetic. We do need to be anxiously engaged in good causes, in our civic duties for example, and to be aware and concerned citizens. We need to understand the principles that our freedoms are based upon and the threats that attack those freedoms. We need to teach our families what patriotism means to us, to tell them how we feel about our country. We need to let our heroes become their heroes. We need to be patriotic, but to be patriotic the way our prophets have taught us to be. In fact, following the counsel of our Church leaders is our first obligation in being true patriots and defenders of liberty. If we pay close attention to their examples of and their teachings about patriotism, we will be more inclined to follow their example.

---

[32]   *More Purity Give Me*, p. 72.

[33]   *HC* 7:603.

[34]   *Man May Know for Himself,* p. 386.

[35]   *GD*, p. 411.

5

The Secularizing of America

There is not an individual upon the earth
but what has within himself ability to save or destroy himself;
and such is the case with nations.

—Brigham Young

Rapid Changes in Modern Times

The old cliché holds true: one thing we can always count on is change. We live in times of significant change. Broadcast journalist, Bill Moyers noted that "change is happening so rapidly and globally that our institutions are not keeping up.[1] The stamina to keep up with such rapid change is often lacking not only institutionally, but also individually, and many people begin to question, *How can I ever survive this world of change?*

---

[1]   *A World of Ideas*, pp. vii-viii.

There is some change that is obviously good; other change is of questionable value. The United States itself is in many ways significantly different than what it was even a decade ago. Unfortunately much of the change that has evolved in American society over the past few years is not for our betterment. Change has happened at the congressional and legislative levels, and at the local civic leadership levels, as well as with the general populace. The moral change the United States has experienced over the past few years is called the secularizing of America.[2]

At a centennial celebration held in Provo, Utah, August 4, 1996, President Gordon B, Hinckley gave a stirring talk on what he called *secularizing America*.[3] "It is of this," said President Hinckley, "that I wish to say a few words...because I feel so strongly about it and because I feel we are paying a terrible price for it." President Hinckley continued: "I have faith in the future of my beloved America," he said, "yet, I am deeply concerned." He addressed such topics as abortion, the crime rate, and diminishing family values. He condemned the attacks being aimed at traditional religious values, and spoke against current anti-religion trends. Concerning these anti-religion trends, Elder Alexander B. Morrison from the first Quorum of Seventy said: "Until recently, prevailing public attitudes toward religion in America were generally respectful."[4]

Ignorance, apathy and irreverence now rule where once reverence and respect dwelt. It seems that on all fronts of society the general attack is against cardinal values that once were heralded as divine. As one author described it, "a subtle but powerful moral transformation which most people intuitively feel but cannot articulate has mutely, yet militantly,

---

[2]   Webster defines secular as "Temporal rather than spiritual: worldly. Not religious or sacred," and secularism as the "belief that religious considerations should be rejected or ignored."

[3]   Provo City Community Centennial Service August 4, 1996. All quotations by President Hinckley used in this chapter are from this address unless otherwise stated.

[4]   *Zion: A Light in the Darkness*, pp. 31-32.

gained momentum in our nation."[5] What has caused such a transformation to take place?

The Moral Code of a Secular Society

"I believe that one of the root causes of the terrible social illness that are running rampant among us," said President Hinckley, "is the almost total secularizing of our public attitudes… Divine law has become a meaningless phrase. What was once so commonly spoken of as sin is now referred to only as poor judgement. Transgression has been replaced by misbehavior." The Lord's Prophet isn't the only one noticing the trends. "[T]he nature of faith is changing," noted one newspaper article. "People are more inclined to question orthodox beliefs, even as they attend church, and they are less committed to conventional religious institutions."[6] And Alexander B. Morrison has noted: "while religious practice in America is flourishing, religious behavior—behavior that comes from deep and abiding religious faith—is much more narrowly based… The ethos of America, its moral, spiritual and aesthetic character and habits—is ill and in serious need of treatment."[7]

Even many churches of the day have taken on reformation to flow with society's great stream. Little do they know that the stream in which they find current is in reality a raging river flowing to the gulf of misery and woe. The river that flows gently to the sea of life, however, is found within the body of the Restoration Church.

One of the ways that certain churches have reformed is that words containing doctrinal annotations have been revised by them to "fit the trends," thus de-emphasizing their real meanings. These secular religionists do not

---

5   *America's State Church*, p. xiii.
6   "God Isn't Dead," The Salt Lake Tribune, December 28, 1998, AA-1.
7   *Zion: A Light in the Darkness*, pp. 35-36.

grasp the concept that our justifying of things will not justify our actions at the day of judgement. What the Lord termed sin four thousand years ago is still sin today. It is the Lord's definition of things that matter, for He is our primal dictionary and out of His book we will be judged.[8]

If we look back on our national history (see chapters 1-3) we will notice that America's success came because of its Christian beliefs and values. She achieved greatness because she was good, and much of her goodness came because of the basic Christian principles taught in her churches. This truth is exemplified in the poetic phraseology of Alexis de Tocqueville. In his book *Democracy in America*, Tocqueville wrote:

> I sought for the greatness and genius of America in her commodious harbors and her ample rivers, and it was not here; in her fertile fields and boundless prairies, and it was not there; in her rich mines and her vast world commerce, and it was not there. *Not until I went to the churches of America and heard her pulpits aflame with righteousness did I understand the secret of her genius and power. America is great because she is good, and if America ever ceases to be good, America will cease to be great.*[9]

When the churches of the day fail in their grand objective—to denounce sin and testify of Christ—they add to the secular wave being heaped upon us now. There used to be a moral code (religious values, beliefs, etc) that governed our nation—a nation founded on the belief of a Supreme Being, a government established with the overruling hand of Providence—but now it seems there is a *no-moral code* that our nation

---

8   "Man has changed again and again, but the mandates from God are still the same as they have always been because the fundamental principles of good behavior are immutable" (David Lawrence, as quoted in *Evans'*, p. 89).
9   As quoted in Ezra Taft Benson, *God, Family, Country: Our Three Great Loyalties*, p. 360.

lives by. If there is no moral code that governs the actions of individuals and conscience then the obvious thing happens: moral law is ignored (the Ten Commandments, the Golden Rule, etc).

We must not blame the churches of the day only for our current secularism. A good question for us to ponder is, *Where ultimately do we place the blame? Is it government, media, our courts of law, parents of families? Who?*

Some of the blame for society's downturn must rest on the shoulders of government leaders and judicial bureaucrats. Numerous decisions have been made in political sanctuaries suggesting that many of our leaders favor secular humanism rather than the ideal Judeo-Christian values that stem from a knowledge that we are accountable beings who will one day stand before the judgement bar of the Great Jehovah. They esteem the popular vote more valuable than an intimate relationship with their Creator, ignoring the reverence that makes such a relationship possible. Stemming from such chaotic root is the prevalent secularism happening today.

Returning to President Hinckley's talk, he related the experience he had of visiting with former British Prime Minister, Lady Margaret Thatcher. "She spoke of the goodness and strength of America," said President Hinckley. Then he related the sad truth that Lady Thatcher observed: "You use the name of Deity in the Declaration of Independence and in the Constitution of the United States, and yet you cannot use it in the school room." President Hinckley confessed, "I heard her make the statement more than once, and I have not forgotten it. This is symptomatic of what I refer to as the secularizing of America. Reverence for the Almighty, gratitude for His beneficent blessings, pleadings for His guidance, are increasingly being dropped from our public discourse." Yet the question must be answered, if not now than later, as novelist E.L. Doctorow posed: "who are we, what are we trying to be, what is our fate, [and] where will we stand in the moral universe when these things are reckoned?"[10]

---

10   As quoted in *A World of Ideas*, p. 83.

Indeed, reckoning must come—and come it will. No nation or individual escapes the scrutinizing eye of the Eternal Judge. All are accountable and all must be judged for their accountability. Such judgement will be placed upon every political officer, every wartime leader, and every lay citizen.

If each person's fate is a future judgement, what of the other questions? Who are we? *Children of God*. What are we trying to be? *A freak of nature*. What is our fate both as a nation and as individuals if we continue to pursue current trends? *A nation or individual(s) without divine approval*. Such Omniscient disapproval has severe consequences, such as the withdrawing of His Spirit (Mormon 5:16; see also Moroni 9:4-6). Without the sustaining Spirit of the Lord to govern the affairs of men and nations, more secularism, more chaotic structure, and more evil envelop society. If indeed the nation now known as the United States of America one day no longer exists, it will be because the people of the United States will have rejected the Source that "made us and [so far] preserved us a nation." Our demise as a nation will not come from a foreign source; it will come from within the country itself. It will be the suicide of a nation.

The Suicide of a Nation (Reaping What We Sow)

When people see not the existence of God in the portrait of human existence, the picture looks bleak indeed. For when people strive to take God out of everything, like society is doing today, what is really happening is a national suicide. It is a slow and painful road the world is traveling, yet it is fatal nonetheless. Instead of heeding unmistakable warnings, as if void of care, the sure Judeo-Christian values that built our nation strong continues to be flooded out by the secular wave of disaster. As a nation both Christian and moral, we are sinking! Abraham Lincoln said in 1837: "If destruction be our lot, we must ourselves be its author and finisher. As a nation of freemen, we must live through all time, or die by suicide."

It is because America has turned its course from a spiritual plateau to a secular slump that President Hinckley warned: "We are shutting the doors...against the God of the universe...we as a nation are forsaking the Almighty." As if this statement by the Lord's Prophet isn't frightening enough, he then said: "and He is forsaking us."

Again the Book of Mormon—that Book of books—is there to remind us what happens when a nation forsakes the Lord and when the Lord forsakes a nation. Is it true that history repeats itself? According to many prophetic leaders, including President Hinckley, the United States today is following the same path of carnality and pride that led to the downfall of both the Jaredite and Nephite nations before us. Like the Nephites in their prime, the American nation has prospered to enormous proportions. She has become the most powerful nation on earth, and surely one of the most wealthy. Freedom has wrung loud and true in the national ear, and patriotism has stemmed from wartime victories. The United States has led the way in science and technology and at one time in religious values. Now, however, it seems this ideal setting has been rearranged. Maybe because of our success, but more readily because we have replaced God with mammon, we have become heady, high-minded, and arrogant. But as Proverbs warns, and as the Book of Mormon teaches so well, "Pride goeth before destruction" (Proverbs 16:18). The Lord's warning to us is, "Beware of pride lest ye become like the Nephites of old" (D&C 38:39).

Perhaps it is the universal sin of pride that is our root problem. Perhaps it is because we have become so powerful that our country possesses the mistaken notion that we don't need God anymore. Could it be that we are like the irreverent man falling from a building who pleads for the Lord to intervene and save him? The jest of the story is that as the man finished his prayer his pant leg caught a flagpole that saved him from a perilous fall. He was then able to grab the pole and climb into the nearest window. Breathing heavily the man said, 'Never mind God, I don't need your help, I saved myself.' The man failed to recognize God's intervention.

Society today may not regard Christianity as "untrue or even unthinkable, merely irrelevant."

We should be proud of our accomplishments, our families, and our country. We should possess a national pride, but we should not be arrogant and have the mistaken notion that we achieved success by ourselves and that we don't need God any more. We should not expend our reliance on God at the cost of undo pride. We cannot save ourselves. Our prophets have emphatically taught, "It is acknowledgment of the Almighty that gives civility and refinement to our actions. It is accountability to Him that brings discipline into our lives. It is gratitude for His gracious favors that takes from us the arrogance to which we are so prone."

The rebuke to all of this is, 'But America isn't that bad. It is still a Christian nation.' Yes, *but is it a Christian nation attested by the actions of our government, our media, and our general frame of mind? Or is it a Christian nation by name only?*

While the United States is still considered a Christian nation, and while it is still the most powerful nation earth—even *the* superpower of the world—somewhere along the road to progressivism we lost something. The virtues once exemplified by the country's political leaders are now seriously lacking. Congress tries desperately to remove every mention of Deity from the public forum, lawless officials hold high rank in government institutions, and while all this goes on "at the top," society cries out in loud protest, 'Pro choice for abortionist!' The crime rate drastically increases every year, and gang violence is becoming the norm in big cities and suburbs alike. The United States faces the problem of illegal immigrants and drug cartels; pornography, prostitution, and many other sexual perversions are constantly displayed to overwhelming odds; idol worship abound as the love for money, power and prestige take their place in the business world, being esteemed more valuable than our neighbor's needs.[11]

---

[11] "No free government can stand," said Andrew Jackson, "without virtue in the people…"

And every individual feels that pangs of these evil influences. Our day is as Paul warned it would be. To Timothy he said:

> This know also, that in the last days perilous times shall come. For men shall be lovers of their own selves, covetous, boasters, proud, blasphemers, disobedient to parents, unthankful, unholy, Without natural affection, trucebreakers, false accusers, incontinent, fierce, despisers of those that are good, Traitors, heady, highminded, lovers of pleasures more than lovers of God; Having a form of godliness, but denying the power thereof... Ever learning, and never able to come to the knowledge of the truth (2 timothy 3:1-7).

The secularism happening today is in fulfillment of the principle, reaping what we sow. It is the Law of the Harvest that the Savior taught as part of His beatitudes: we can only harvest that which we have planted.

Recently while taking a mass communications course my professor played a videotape that showed media students how drastically television (society's perception and tolerance) had changed in just a little over forty years. The video lasted no more than fifteen minutes and contained footage from one top-ranking sitcom in each decade from the 1950's to the 1990's. The sitcoms were: *I Love Lucy* (1950's), *The Dick Van Dyke Show* (1960's), *The Mary Tyler Moore Show* (1970's), *Cheers* (1980's), and *Seinfeld* (1990's).

The first two sitcoms mentioned here were clean, family oriented shows. There was no vulgarity or crudeness associated with them. If the camera panned a bedroom, there were two twin beds displayed to hide any suggestion of sex. In the 1970's, however, we begin to see a shift in certain values. Mary Tyler Moore played a liberal-minded, working woman. The show coincided with the equal rights movement of the day, as Mary portrayed a woman trying to prove herself in the work field. The set for *Cheers* was, of all places, a bar. Much of the content of this show was centered on sex and liberalism. The twin beds shown in *I Love Lucy* and *The Dick Van Dyke Show* were replaced with queen beds with people in them—unclothed even! The show *Seinfeld* ranked number one in the 1990's until it was cancelled in 1998. *Seinfeld* talked easily of sex, orgasms, gay and lesbian issues, and masturbation. Quite a contrast between the clean and reserved, yet number one sitcom of all time, *I Love Lucy*.

The example presented here brings up myriad other issues: does society change first and then television changes to reflect the way society has changed? Or does television change first, which then influences society's values? Whatever the answer, the result is no less severe. President Hinckley emphatically taught that America is "forgetting God." That is the root of our problems today. President Hinckley said:

> *Today we face challenges we have scarcely known in the past.* We have come through wars, both civil and international, with victory and found peace. Now we are a people of contention, with strident and accusatory voices heard in argument across the nation. We rose from scratch to become the greatest industrial power in the history of the earth. Now we have lost much of our competitive edge and have seen other nations move ahead of us in various fields in both research and production. We spend millions upon millions of our resources in litigation one against another. Our spiritual power is sapped by a floodtide of pornography, by a debilitating epidemic of the use of narcotics and drugs that destroy both body and mind. *We are forgetting God, whose commandments we have put aside and obey not. In all too many ways we have substituted human sophistry for the wisdom of the Almighty.*[12]

---

12   As quoted in *The Spirit of America*, pp. 32-33.

Is It Too Late For America?

If God is forsaking America, is it too late for us as a nation? Do we have any hope of again obtaining heaven's blessings? If so, how do we go about it? Professor Hugh Nibley has analyzed the following:

> The fatal symptom of our day is not that men do wrong—they always have—and commit crimes, and even recognize their wrong-doings as foolish and unfortunate, but that they have no intention of repenting, while God has told us that the first rule that he has given the human race is that all men everywhere must repent.[13]

It is one thing—bad enough as it is—to forsake God in the first place, but it is worse to continue forsaking Him by never repenting. It is interesting that the answer to America's problems—the world's problems for that matter—already exists. The remedy is the good news of salvation, the glad tidings of the restoration, the fullness of the gospel of Jesus Christ. To remedy society, we must remedy the individual. We cannot come unto Christ as a nation until we come unto Him as individuals and families. A plethora of examples illustrate that the actions of one individual can have a tremendous impact on a larger population, for either good or bad.

During the dark days of the Civil War, President Abraham Lincoln, a reverent man, called upon the country to hold a day of fasting and prayer. His wisdom, as well as his reverence, permeated his injunction to the nation. He said:

---

[13]   *Of All Things*, p. 189.

It is the duty of nations as well as men to own their dependence upon the overruling power of God, to confess their sins and transgressions in humble sorrow, yet with assured hope that genuine repentance will lead to mercy and pardon, and to recognize the sublime truth, announced in the holy scriptures and proven by all history, that those nations only are blessed whose God is the Lord.[14]

The Psalmist, teaching an everlasting principle, penned these significant words: "Blessed is the nation whose God is the Lord" (Psalms 33:12). May we all take more seriously our responsibility to society and carefully utilize the opportunities which are ours to help make this a "blessed nation."

---

[14]   As quoted in *The Spirit of America*, p. 7; original spelling corrected.

6
Family—The Keystone of Society

Family time should be found for cultivating that better part,
that one thing needful—true, spiritual development.

—James E. Talmage

The nation is no stronger than the homes of the people,
and the Church is no stronger in its practical aspects
and in the faith and devotion of its members
than the homes of the people.

—Gordon B. Hinckley

Society vs. the Family

One of the most drastic ways we can help change society is by strengthening our own families. The Church of Jesus Christ of Latter-day Saints has recently televised major Public Service Announcements with the theme, *Family*. The subtitle to the theme is in the format of a question: *Isn't it about time?* These Public Service Announcements are more pertinent to our day than ever.

With so many outside demands pulling us away from the home, crucial time and energy with the family is a must for any healthy life. The last days do not get easier; they only get tougher, with ever increasing demands pulling from work, school, church assignments, piano recitals, and little league. These and similar activities are all good in and of themselves, but taken as a whole they can be very stressful on any marriage or family. Our secular society makes it near to impossible anymore for the wife to stay home. This is a serious detriment for the couple who desires the *ideal*, often termed old-fashioned, format of marriage and home life.

Society's demands had at once affected my own family. The financial situation we found ourselves in forced my wife into the work place to help supplement our income. Both of us worked full-time which caused our young son to be bounced around from grandma's house on certain days to neighborhood baby-sitters on other days. Often my wife's work schedule and mine were totally opposite of each other's. This hectic routine went on for some time, and it seemed we were never spending any family time together. One day we both got fed up with it and concluded that the only way we would be able to spend "quantity" time together was if we took sick leave from our jobs. Neither of us had very much vacation time so a trip was out of the question. As crazy as this may sound, taking sporadic sick days helped supplement our family time together.

On one of the mornings of our alleged "sick days," my wife and I were watching a rebroadcast of a conference address given by President Ezra Taft Benson. After President Benson's address, the Church's Public Service Announcement aired. I meditated on the ad, which made me better understand the precarious situation my family and I were in. I remember saying something like this to my wife: "It's pretty bad when we feel we have to call into work with an alleged illness just to be able to spend time as a family." Time, it has been said, is a most precious commodity, more valuable than riches. If one truly had time to do everything one ever wanted to do, that person would be rich indeed. How much richer would that person be, however, if his or her time were devoted to the family!

This chapter is not written to prompt people to call into work with an alleged illness, but it is written to promote the importance of the family unit—the only stable unit in a society full of instability. *It is an undermined truth that the stable family unit is the keystone to a healthy and functional society. Remove the keystone and society falls apart.* President Gordon B. Hinckley addressed the issue as follows:

> One need not, of course, read statistics to recognize a moral decay that seems to be going on all about us. It is evident in the easy breakup of marriages, in widespread infidelity, in the growth of youth gangs, in the increased use of drugs and the epidemic spread of AIDS, and in a growing disregard for the lives and property of others. It is seen in the defacement of private and public property with graffiti, which destroys beauty and is an insult to art. It is expressed in the language of the gutter, which is brought into our homes.
>
> The endless sex and violence of network TV, the trash of so many motion pictures, the magnified sensuality found in much of modern literature, the emphasis on sex education, a widespread breakdown of law and order—all are manifestations of this decay.
>
> What is the answer? Is there any way to change the course of the ethical and moral slide we are experiencing? I believe there is.
>
> What is happening is simply an ugly expression of the declining values of our society. Those who are concerned with the problem advocate more legal regulation, large appropriations for increased police forces, tax increases to build additional jails and prisons. These may be needed to deal with the present problems. They may help in the near term. But they will be only as a bandage too small for the sore. They help in taking care of the fruits, but they

will not get at the roots. In searching for remedies, we speak of a greater work that must be done in our schools. But educators have largely abdicated their responsibility for teaching values. The Church is looked to—this and all other churches.... We as a church are doing much, very much, and I think we are accomplishing much. But it is not enough.

When all is said and done, the primary place in building a value system is in the homes of the people.[1]

President Hinckley's words are what the Lord's prophets have always taught. "Remember, the family is one of God's greatest fortresses against the evils of our day," said Ezra Taft Benson. "Help keep your family strong and close and worthy of our Father in Heaven's blessings. As you do, you will receive faith and strength, which will bless your lives forever."[2]

One of the first steps to a healthy and stable family life, as the Church's theme suggests, is about *time*. Time for husbands and wives; time for fathers and sons; time for mothers and daughters; time for brothers and sisters; time for parent[s] and child[ren].

What the Lord and His Prophets Have Said Concerning Family

The family unit has always been important to the Lord and His Church. When all is said and done with even the Church organization pales in significance next to the family unit. Prophets have repeatedly proclaimed "Family First." Listed below are some quotes from the Lord and His ancient and modern prophets concerning the family. Some quotes deal with the responsibilities of family members, other quotes give wise

---

[1]   As quoted in *Families*, pp. 49-50.
[2]   *Come, Listen to a Prophet's Voice*, p. 2.

counsel to help make our families stronger. Some quotes deal with the importance of family time, and still others speak of the eternal nature of the family unit and the importance of families in our Heavenly Father's plan of salvation. Salvation after all *is* a family affair.

—*Old Testament*

And Adam gave names to all cattle, and to the fowl of the air, and to every beast of the field; but for Adam there was not found an help meet for him.

And the Lord God caused a deep sleep to fall upon Adam, and he slept: and he took one of [Adam's] ribs, and closed up the flesh instead thereof;

And the rib, which the Lord God had taken from man, made he a woman, and brought her unto the man.

And Adam said, *This is now bone of my bones, and flesh of my flesh*: she shall be called Woman, because she was taken out of Man.

Therefore shall a man leave his father and his mother, and shall *cleave* unto his wife: and they shall be one flesh.

And they were both naked, the man and his wife, and were not ashamed (Genesis 1:20-25).

Live joyfully with the wife whom [God] hath given thee… (Ecclesiastes 9:9).

[W]oman [is] to be a joyful mother of children (Psalms 113:9).

And all thy children shall be taught of the LORD; and great shall be the peace of thy children (Isaiah 54:13).

—*New Testament*

Husbands, love your wives, even as Christ also loved the church, and gave himself for it (Ephesians 5:25).

Nevertheless let every one of you in particular so love his wife even as himself; and the wife see that she reverence her husband (Ephesians 5:33).

For this cause shall a man leave his father and mother, and cleave to his wife; And they twain shall be one flesh: so then they are no more twain, but one flesh.

What therefore God hath joined together, let not man put asunder (Mark 10:7-9).

—*Book of Mormon*

I, Nephi, having been born of *goodly parents,* therefore I was taught somewhat in all the learning of my father (1 Nephi 1:1).

Now they never had fought, yet they did not fear death; and they did think more upon the liberty of their fathers than they did upon their lives; yea, they had been taught *by their mothers*, that if they did not doubt, God would deliver them.

And they rehearsed unto me the words of their mothers, saying: We do not doubt our mothers knew it (Alma 56:47-48).

And ye will not suffer your children that they go hungry, or naked; neither will ye suffer that they transgress the laws of God, and fight and quarrel one with another, and serve the devil, who is the master of sin, or who is the evil spirit which hath been spoken of by our fathers, he being an enemy to all righteousness.

But ye will teach them to walk in the ways of truth and soberness; ye will teach them to love one another, and to serve one another (Mosiah 4:14).

—*Doctrine & Covenants*

And again, inasmuch as parents have children in Zion, or in any of her stakes which are organized, that teach them not to understand the doctrine of repentance, faith in Christ the Son of the living God, and of baptism and the gift of the Holy Ghost by the laying on of hands, when eight years old, the sin be upon the heads of the parents.

And their children shall be baptized for the remission of their sins when eight years old, and receive the laying on of hands.

And they shall also teach their children to pray, and to walk uprightly before the Lord.

And the inhabitants of Zion shall also observe the Sabbath day to keep it holy (D&C 68:25-29).

All children have claim upon their parents for their maintenance until they are of age (D&C 83:4).

—*Joseph Smith*

Time and experience, however, are the only safe remedies against such evils. There are many teachers but perhaps not many fathers.[3]

---

3   *TPJS*, p. 144.

—*Brigham Young*

If the law of Christ becomes the tradition of this people, the children will be brought up according to the law of the celestial kingdom, else they are not brought up in the way they should go.[4]

If parents will continually set before their children examples worthy of their imitation and the approval of our Father in Heaven, they will turn the current, and the tide of feelings of their children, and they, eventually, will desire righteousness more than evil.[5]

—*John Taylor*

We should live together in love. There should be union in every family circle and harmony in every neighborhood and city. We should be cleanly in our persons, in our dress, and in our habitations and surroundings. Industry should be habitual with the adults of our community, and the rising generation should be taught its lessons and be impressed with its value as a means of happiness. God has given us the earth as a dwelling place, and when mankind live as they should do, it is a delightful residence.... *A well-ordered lovely home, in which peace and goodwill prevail is a place of perpetual delight to those who reside there, whether old or young.... By furnishing means of instruction, amusement, and enjoyment at home, parents can...tie their children to them by bonds of affection that can never be broken. In after years those children will think of that home as the brightest and dearest spot in their memories; in their minds it will always be surrounded by a heavenly halo.*[6]

---

4   *DBY,* p. 207.
5   Ibid. p. 208.
6   *The Gospel Kingdom: Writings and Discourses of John Taylor,* pp. 283-284.

Husbands, do you love your wives and treat them right, or do you think that you yourselves are some great moguls who have a right to crowd upon them? They are given to you as a part of yourself, and you ought to treat them with all kindness, with mercy and longsuffering, and not be harsh and bitter, or in anyway desirous to display your authority. Then, you wives, treat your husbands right, and try to make them happy and comfortable. Endeavor to make your homes a little heaven, and try to cherish the good Spirit of God. Then let us parents train up our children in the fear of God and teach them the laws of life. If you do, we will have peace in our bosoms, peace in our families, and peace in our surroundings.[7]

—*Wilford Woodruff*

Love your fathers and mothers, appreciate and enjoy their society while you are with them, for you will soon enough be called to part with them, and if you live to see that day you will see the time when you will fully appreciate their society and know the worth of their counsel.[8]

Obey your parents in all things and comfort their hearts, for you have the power to do this. When they are weary and pressed with the cares of life, seek to ease their burdens and smile upon them in their hours of sorrow and you will cast a charm of joy and peace around them which they cannot obtain from any other source.

Be kind to your brothers and sisters and all with whom you associate; kind words and good manners will cost you nothing and will add greatly to the happiness of those around you. Be true to

---

7   Ibid. p. 284.
8   *The Discourses of Wilford Woodruff*, p. 266-267.

yourselves by doing right in all things, by improving well your time and talents, by being wise, virtuous, and good. Be true to your God by keeping his commandments and doing his will, for he holds your destiny and the destiny of your parents and of all men in his own hands and he will reward all according to their works, whether they be good or evil, and all will be amply paid for doing well.—JH 2, May 1, 1857.

Be happy, be contented, enjoy the days of your youth, enjoy your peaceful homes, enjoy the society of your parents, brothers, and sisters while you have an opportunity, for the days of your youth will soon be gone.[9]

—*Lorenzo Snow*

The men ought to be more fatherly at home, possessing finer feelings in reference to their wives and children, neighbors and friends, more kindly and godlike. When I go into a family I do admire to see the head of that family administering to it as a man of God, kind and gentle, filled with the Holy Ghost and with the wisdom and understanding of heaven.[10]

—*Joseph F. Smith*

To be a successful father or a successful mother is greater than to be a successful general or a successful statesman. One is universal and eternal greatness, the other is ephemeral.[11]

Neither are the relationships that exist, or should exist, between parents and children, and between children and parents, of an

---

[9]　Ibid. p. 267.
[10]　*Teachings of Lorenzo Snow*, pp. 135-136.
[11]　*GD*, p. 285.

ephemeral nature, nor of a temporal character. They are of eternal consequence, reaching beyond the veil, in spite of all that we do.... For this reason, God has guarded this institution by the most severe penalties...[12]

Our associations are not exclusively intended for this life, for time, as we distinguish it from eternity. We live for time and for eternity. *We form associations and relations for time and all eternity. Our affections and our desires are found fitted and prepared to endure not only throughout the temporal or mortal life, but through all eternity.* Who are there besides the Latter-day Saints who contemplate the thought that beyond the grave we will continue in the family organization? the father, the mother, and children recognizing each other in the relations which they owe to each other and in which they stand to each other? this family organization being a unit in the great and perfect organization of God's work, and all destined to continue throughout time and eternity?[13]

—Heber J. Grant

Faith is a gift of God. If we seek for faith the Lord blesses us with that faith. It becomes a gift from Him, and we are promised that if we will do the will of the Father we shall know of the doctrine. If we as parents will so order our lives that our children will know and realize in their hearts that we are in very deed Latter-day Saints, that we actually know what we are talking about, they, by seeking after the Lord, will get the same testimony.[14]

---

12 Ibid. pp. 272-273.
13 Ibid. pp. 348.
14 *Gospel Standards*, p. 145.

I pray that your example may be such that your children will live the gospel of Jesus Christ, because that is of more value than anything else in the world.[15]

—*George Albert Smith*

Grateful should we be for a knowledge of the eternity of the marriage covenant. If in this life only had we hope, we would indeed be of all men most miserable. *The assurance that our relationship here as parents and children, as husbands and wives will continue in heaven, and that this is but the beginning of a great and glorious kingdom that our Father has destined we shall inherit on the other side, fills us with hope and joy.* One of the greatest evidence to me of the divinity of this work is that it teaches there is eternal life on the other side, and that there will be a reunion there of the loved ones who have known each other here. Consequently, as parents, we may well be patient and loving toward our children, for they will eternally abide with us on the other side, if we and they are faithful. The few years that we live here may be regarded as a time in which we become acquainted, but, when we mingle in the other life, we will know each other better than we have here.[16]

I fear that sometimes we neglect them. I wonder tonight if the men who are here, who have come to this great conference to worship God, who are here to be instructed under the influence of the Spirit of the Lord,—have left homes, left households in which there is a family of children besides the wife. I am asking myself the question, "How many of you who are here tonight,

---

[15]　Ibid. p. 156.
[16]　*TGAS*, p. 110; emphasis added.

before you came here to wait upon the Lord, put your arms around the woman who stood by your side, the mother of your children, and told her that you were grateful that she would keep the home-fires burning when you couldn't be there?" I wonder if we appreciate the daughters of God as he appreciates them. Do we treasure their virtues and their faith and their devotion and their motherhood as our Heavenly Father does?[17]

—David O. McKay

The principle reason for marriage is to rear a family. Failure to do so is one of the conditions that cause love to wilt and eventually die.[18]

—Joseph Fielding Smith

It is written in the scriptures: "For this cause (the Gospel) I bow the knees unto the Father of our Lord Jesus Christ, of whom the *whole family* in heaven and earth is named." (Eph. 3:14-15) So we see that there is a family organization in heaven, and part of it on earth, but in both places it is named after God the Father of Jesus Christ.[19]

Logically there can be no marriage without the family. Nor can there be full peace, joy and blessing in the kingdom of God, unless parents and children are eternally bound by covenant to each other.[20]

---

[17] Ibid. p. 112.
[18] *Gospel Ideals*, p. 466.
[19] *The Pathway to Perfection*, p. 256.
[20] Ibid. 253.

—*Harold B. Lee*

I believe the parents of our children nowadays need to be taught the proper way of bringing up the Latter-day Saint child: more family nights, more family activity, *more time together*, greater emphasis in the home on the importance of sacred ordinances.[21]

—*Spencer W. Kimball*

Imagine how much richer our family life would be if our spouses and children were to receive a few more minutes of individual attention each month![22]

—*Ezra Taft Benson*

Again, are we holding family home evenings each week? Your immediate results may seem far from ideal at times, but *by holding weekly family home evenings, as we have been counseled, we help to perfect that eternal family unit.*[23]

God intended the family to be eternal. With all my soul, I testify to the truth of that declaration. May He bless us to strengthen our homes and the lives of each family member so that in due time we can report to our Heavenly Father in His celestial home that we are all there—father, mother, sister, brother, all who hold each other dear. Each chair is filled. We are all back home.[24]

---

[21] *THBL*, p. 261; emphasis added.
[22] *TSWK*, p. 177.
[23] *TETB*, pp. 178-179.
[24] Ibid. p. 493.

—*Howard W. Hunter*

A man who holds the priesthood regards the family as ordained of God. Your leadership of the *family is your most important and sacred responsibility.*[25]

To reach success in the family, parents must have love and respect for each other. Husbands, the bearers of the priesthood, should hold their wives in the highest esteem before their children, and wives should love and support their husbands. In return, the children will have love for their parents and for each other. The home will then become a hallowed place where the principles of the gospel can be best lived and where the Spirit of the Lord can dwell. To be a successful father or a successful mother is far greater than to rise to leadership or high places in business, government, or worldly affairs. *Home may seem commonplace at times with its routine duties, yet its success should be the greatest of all our pursuits in life.*[26]

—*Gordon B. Hinckley*

I think every officer in the Church, all of us in this Church, serve in a part-time capacity and have a fourfold responsibility. One, they have a responsibility to their families, *to see that their families have a measure of their time.* What should it profit a man if he gain the whole world and lose his own, paraphrasing the Savior's words. Every man has a responsibility toward his family. None of us can evade that.... *We must have time to be with family. That is basic and it is fundamental.*[27]

---

25   *Teachings of Howard W. Hunter*, p. 154, emphasis added.
26   Ibid. p. 156; emphasis added.
27   *TGBH*, p. 33.

You have to sit down now and look at your resources. *The major resource in this matter* [family] *is time.*[28]

---

[28]　Ibid. emphasis added.

7

America in an Age of Internationalism

In order for a man to be a good neighbor within his community,
he had better first love his own family
before he tries to save the neighborhood.

—Ezra Taft Benson

The twentieth century has been labeled an epoch of massive technological growth, and rightly so. For countless centuries mankind has plummeted along life's highway with few world-changing advancements. Sure we have the great mysteries of ancient civilizations. The pyramid, for example, has stunned the modern world for years. We ask ourselves, *How did these ancients ever build such monuments without giant caterpillars or cranes?* Countless other wonders have boggled the modernists. Take for example the statue of Zeus at Olympia, or the Temple of Artemis at Ephesos, or still the Mausoleum at Halicarnassus. Each of these has become one of the wonders of the Ancient World.

The light of Christ that every person born into this world freely possesses as a conscience has guided mankind through the ages to great heights, inspiring him to make improvements where needed. For the most part, however, the world had traveled in chaotic structure along the road to progressivism. That is, of course, until the dispensation of the fullness of times, which opened to the world in the spring of 1820. Then the heavens were again parted and God spoke again with man. Since 1820 the world has experienced remarkable, unprecedented growth unlike any other epoch in world history. Whereas before the world was knit as a huge, ephemeral planet too big to explore every clime, today the world has become much smaller with satellite dishes and computer keyboards. Truly we live in an age of internationalism, and America leads the way in such a time as this.

With the remarkable growth of the sciences and technologies has come also a political and military growth that has necessitated certain change in the political arena. Much of this is with regard to foreign policy and how we as a nation interact with the other nations of the globe. But under the necessity of such change, should we as a nation withdraw ourselves from the original principles of American foreign policy as formulated by our wise Founding Fathers? Can the United States be affiliated with the world body organization, the United Nations, and still remain an independent and sovereign nation? How much sovereignty as a nation are we willing to give up to be part of the UN? Will the United Nations bring world peace? This chapter will analyze these and other questions related to the United Nations and America foreign policy issues.

The United Nations and World Peace

The League of Nations

During the height of World War I, President Woodrow Wilson dramatized his desire for a one-world government. "I hate this war!" he said. "I hate all war and the only thing I care about on earth is the peace I am going to make at the end of it."[1] Soon after World War I, Wilson and other world leaders decided upon fourteen political points to establish mutual agreement between nations, one being the General Association of Nations. The overall plan that was formulated was named the *League of Nations*.

> Under the leadership of Wilson, the Covenant of the League of Nations was signed in less than four months. The Covenant, or constitution, provided for a Council composed of the United States, England, France, Italy, Japan, and four rotating members. It also created an Assembly where all nations' members could vote. In the Covenant, members promised to reduce arms to a minimum. They also promised not to trade with warring nations as a way of forcing them to stop fighting. The Covenant also established many international organizations, such as a World Court. Waving a copy of the Covenant, Wilson said, "This document is the condemnation of war...*people can now live together in friendship.*"[2]

Suffice it to be said that the League of Nations failed in its proposed mission. The very thing the *League* was supposed to prevent happened in 1939, the beginning of World War II.

---

[1]   As quoted in Harold and Geraldine Woods, *The United Nations*, p. 7.
[2]   Ibid.

The United Nations and Its Charter

By 1945 leaders of the world sought new opportunity to create a world government. The desired goal was as before: to bring harmony and unity between the nations of the globe. The deficiencies of the League of Nations that caused its demise were in 1945 plainly seen in retrospect. Just as the Second World War was coming to a close, and after three years of planning and debate, on June 16, 1945, fifty-one nations signed the *United Nations Charter*.[3] The *United Nations*, the leaders said, would amend the deficiencies of the *League* if each country pulled together and supported the new organization. Former Emperor of Ethiopia, Haile Selassie, said the United Nations "reposes the best—perhaps the last—hope for the peaceful survival of mankind."[4] However, while leaders of the world applauded the new agreement, leaders of the Church condemned it. While it was approaching the time of its inauguration, Apostle J. Rueben Clark Jr. spoke vehemently

---

3   The Preamble to the United Nations Charter reads as follows:
     WE THE PEOPLES OF THE UNITED NATIONS DETERMINED to save succeeding generations from the scourge of war, which twice in our lifetime has brought untold sorrow to mankind, and to reaffirm faith in fundamental human rights, in the dignity and worth of the human person, in the equal rights of men and women and of nations large and small, and to established conditions under which justice and respect for the obligations arising from treatise and other sources of international law can be maintained, and to promote social progress and better standards of life in larger freedom, AND FOR THESE ENDS to practice tolerance and live together in peace with one another as good neighbors, and to unite our strength to maintain international peace and security, and to ensure, by the acceptance of principles and the institution of methods, that armed force shall not be used, save in the common interest, and to employ international machinery for the promotion of the economic and social advancement of all peoples, HAVE RESOLVED TO COMBINE OUR EFFORTS TO ACCOMPLISH THESE AIMS. Accordingly our respective Governments, through representatives assembled in the city of San Francisco, who have exhibited their full powers found to be in good and due form, have agreed to the present Charter of the United Nations and do hereby establish an international organization to be known as the United Nations.
4   As quoted in *Internationalism: Opposing Viewpoints*, p. 72.

against the UN Charter. "There seems no reason to doubt," he said, "that such real approval as the Charter has among the people is based upon the belief that if the Charter is put into effect, wars will end...." With apostolic insight President Clark then said:

> The Charter will not certainly end war. Some will ask—why not? In the first place, *there is no provision in the Charter itself that contemplates ending war. It is true the Charter provides for force to bring peace, but such use of force is itself war*.... It is true the Charter is built to prepare for war, not to promote peace.... *The* [United Nations] *Charter is a war document not a peace document.*[5]

One author, writing on the United Nations observed: "Of all the cliches that have played a role in the historical development of the United Nations, none has been used more extensively than the claim that the UN is man's last and best hope for peace. Even today it is difficult to locate a pro-UN article, speech, or book that does not emphasize this central theme. Despite the fact that not a single provision in the UN Charter contemplates an end to war."[6] Continuing his analysis of the UN Charter, President Clark detailed:

> *Not only does the Charter Organization not prevent future wars, but it makes it practically certain that we will have future wars,* and as to such wars it takes from us [the United States] the power to declare them, to choose the side on which we will fight, to determine what forces and military equipment we shall use in the war, *and to control and command our sons who do the fighting.*[7]

---

5   As quoted in Ezra Taft Benson, *An Enemy Hath Done This,* p. 160
6   Robert W. Lee, *The United Nations Conspiracy,* p. 33.
7   As quoted in Ezra Taft Benson, *An Enemy Hath Done This,* p. 161.

One event will be related here, though there are many, which give credit to President Clark's statement quoted above: In August of 1995, Army Specialist Michael New, while stationed in Germany, learned that his unit was to be deployed to Macedonia as part of a UN assignment. As part of this contingent "American soldiers were required to wear UN insignia and serve under a foreign UN commander." New opposed this requirement, saying, "I have a problem with that, because I am not UN." New reported, "I explained this to my lieutenant and told him, 'Sir, I don't think I should have to wear a UN armband or a UN beret. I'm enlisted in the U.S. Army; I am not a UN soldier. I have taken no vow to the UN.'" But, said New to his lieutenant, "'I have taken an oath to defend the Constitution of the United States of America from enemies foreign and domestic... Where does my oath say I have to wear UN insignia?'" In response to New's avowal, his lieutenant said: "'Well, soldier, you enlisted in the Army, and the oath you took was to obey orders from your chain of command and we're saying—WEAR IT!'" New was informed that if he did not comply with wearing the UN insignia he would face a court martial. But standing by his conviction New related, "I believe the UN is a foreign power no different than a foreign government... I would not wear a Russian uniform or salute a Russian flag... For the same reason, I won't wear [the UN insignia]."[8]

The reader can determine in his or her own mind whether he or she supports Michael New in his resolve or not. This one instance, however, substantiates very well what President Clark said more than fifty years ago: that "the [UN] Charter Organization...takes from us [the United States] the power...to control and command our sons who do the fighting."

Elder Ezra Taft Benson said: "Sovereignty for a nation is hard to come by, and even more difficult to retain. It cannot be shared, for then sovereignty becomes something else, and, for lack of a better word, when sovereignty

---

8   See "I Am Not a UN Soldier." *The New American*, October 2, 1995, p. 5.

is lessened the end product is internationalism. Sovereignty is neither more nor less than self-government. And American self-government is blueprinted in the Constitution."⁹ But despite the knowing facts, "The United Nations has become the recipient of so much praise and favorable publicity, most of us have come to regard it as the embodiment of our own hopes for peace and a better future world." The tendency is to believe that the UN is a great world physician that can remedy every problem. But the UN is neither our physician nor our psychologist. The "better future world" as supposed to be created by the UN will never come about; it is an illusion, a dreamscape.

It is a truth easily substantiated that since 1945 when the United Nations came into power there have been hundreds of conflicts across the globe: wars in such places as Korea, Vietnam, Kuwait, Bosnia and Kosovo to name only a select few. *The UN has not repressed aggression.*¹⁰ Yet advocates of the UN claim, "but these conflicts have not resulted in a Third World

---

9   *An Enemy Hath Done This*, p. 99.

10   If it is true that the United Nations is only an illusion, a dreamscape for hopeful world peace, then where in reality will peace ever be found? Will peace ever be made available through any man-made organization? Or does mortal man try in vein to accomplish the miraculous? Concerning the peace treatise of the latter-days, President George Q. Cannon said in 1863: "Elaborate and beautiful theories may be constructed, but they will crumble to atoms before the stern logic of facts and leave those who adopt them in a worse predicament than they were in before they attempted to put them into practice. While man remains as he is and as he has been since God's revelations and direct manifestations and guidance have been withheld from him [since the Great Apostasy], *all such schemes as these for Peace or International Congresses must be barren of all good and permanent results*" (*Gospel Truth*, p. 45; emphasis added). President Cannon also said concerning the aversion of warfare: "War is one of the scourges which man, by his sinfulness, has brought upon himself. *There is one way—and but one way—to avert it and that is for the people to obey God's commands, through whose power alone can this and all other threatened evils be stayed*" (Ibid. emphasis added). If the world does not repent, "They are to be wasted away by war…" (Ibid. p. 44) "until the consumption decreed hath made a full end of all nations" (D&C 87:6).

War. The United Nations has made the difference."[11] Perhaps this is true; I am not one to say it is not. But the simple truth of the whole matter hangs in the balance: the Lord's prophets have warned for various reasons against America's involvement in the world body organization; reasons that many of us may not clearly see or understand at the present time.

American Foreign Policy

The foreign policy issue has such drastic and complicated appeal in the political arena. On the pulpit of the past, for example, is President George Washington's proposal of isolationism as the best policy for the United States to follow with regard to other nations. On the podium of the twenty-first century, however, advocates say isolationism no longer applies. Indeed times have changed, and so has America's role as it emerged as a super power. The United States does have power, influence, and responsibility to the rest of the world, of this there is no doubt. But what exactly *is* America's responsibility to the world?

George Washington's Great Rule of Conduct

George Washington's farewell address, as is printed in the *American Daily Advertiser*, September 19, 1796, implied that "The great rule of conduct for us, in regard to foreign nations, is in extending our commercial relations to have with them as little political connection as possible. So far as we have already formed engagements, let them be fulfilled with perfect good faith. Here let us stop."[12]

---

[11]   Clark Eichelberger, former National Director of the American Association for the United Nations, as quoted in *The United Nations Conspiracy*, p. 40.

[12]   As quoted in *Isolationism: Opposing Viewpoints*, p. 27.

In Washington's day the newly founded country rallied to support the President's impassioned teaching of isolationism. The concept became the over-riding principle in the emerging years of American foreign relations. It helped shape the future of the American nation, which nation in turn helped change the world. It seemed as though Washington's theory was here to stay. It was the dream-quest of sovereignty, the theoretic abode of peace lovers. Washington also said:

> I have always given it as my decided opinion that no nation has a right to intermeddle in the internal concerns of another; that every one had a right to form and adopt whatever government they liked best to live under themselves; and that, if this country could, *consistently* with its engagements, *maintain* a strict neutrality and thereby preserve peace, it was bound to do so by motives of policy, interest, and every other consideration.[13]

The questions that have risen since Washington's time have dealt with the consistency problem. One reporter noted that "The American people have never accepted traditional geopolitics or pure balance-of-power calculations as sufficient reason to expend national treasure or to dispatch American soldiers to foreign lands.... The American people want their country's foreign policy rooted in idealpolitik as well as realpolitik."[14] While serving as Secretary of Agriculture under President Dwight D. Eisenhower, Elder Ezra Taft Benson of the Quorum of Twelve Apostles delivered an address on the topic of American Foreign Policy. In his address Elder Benson suggested the correct measures of foreign policy as follows:

> To protect our people from international theft, we must enter into agreements with other nations to abide by certain rules

---

[13] As quoted in *An Enemy Hath Done This*, p. 151; emphasis added.
[14] *Foreign Affairs*, Nov/Dec 1996, p. 49.

regarding trade, exchange of currency, enforcement of contracts, patent rights, etc. To protect our people against involuntary servitude of the loss of personal freedom on the international level, we must be willing to use our military might to help even one of our citizens no matter where he might be kidnapped or enslaved....

[But] *Certainly we must avoid becoming entangled in a web of international treaties whose terms and clauses might reach inside our own borders and restrict our freedoms here at home.*

This is the defensive role of government expressed in international terms. Interestingly enough, these three aspects of national defense also translate directly into the three aspects of national sovereignty: military, economic and political.[15]

Elder Benson, who drastically opposed the United Nations and *entangling alliances*, received favored support for his conclusions from President David O. McKay, J. Rueben Clark, Jr., and Marion G. Romney—all civic leaders, and all apostolic witnesses of Jesus Christ.

New Theories to Replace the Old

Soon after World War II drastic measures were taken which isolated the isolationists and their theories. In 1945 the world was seen in a new light. The dropping of the atomic bomb on Hiroshima heightened military advancements not just in the States, but in the major countries across the globe. The world had become a much smaller place, which necessitated change with regard to foreign policy. Isolationism was to see its demise. One book that describes America's change from an isolationist country to a dominant player in world affairs, says:

---

[15]　*An Enemy Hath Done*, pp. 152-153; emphasis added.

World War II ended with America's dropping the atomic bombs on Japan. The beginning of the atomic age was only one aspect of a vastly changed world. Most of the powerful nations that had competed for world influence prior to the war—Japan, Great Britain, France, Germany, Italy—were so devastated by war as to be no longer significant players on the world scene, unable even to maintain their colonial empires in Africa and Asia. The United States found itself in the position of being one of two superpowers in the entire world. The other was the Soviet Union....

Disputes over American foreign policy now focused on U.S.-Soviet relations. Some Americans, such as former vice president Henry Wallace, argued that the United States should work to build on its cooperative wartime relationship with the Soviet Union and create a system of collective security based on the League of Nations model. Others, such as diplomat George Kennan, argued that the United States should confront and "contain" the expansionist and ideologically dangerous Soviet Union, and should, in order to achieve that goal, enter into alliance with other countries. Neither side advocated U.S. withdrawal or neutrality in world affairs.[16]

What happened next? "As a result the United States took a series of actions that would have been unthinkable fifty—or even ten—years earlier. Rather than repeat its refusal to join the League of Nations, it instead joined the United Nations, a new international organization created to replace Woodrow Wilson's failed dream."[17] Since 1945 the United Nations has played a major role in American foreign policy issues.

---

[16]   *Isolationism: Opposing Viewpoints,* pp. 206-207.

[17]   Ibid. p. 207.

Full Circle

Here we come full-circle to the topic of American Foreign Policy. It is a heated debate in the political arena and on the world scene. The United Nations, so it seems, is here to stay as a stable symbol of this world's effort for peace. It is a political fact, however, that we cannot fulfill healthy foreign policy objectives when we are a branch of the world body organization. If we are to maximize our independence and sovereignty as a nation we cannot adopt a foreign flag or foreign constitution. Yet this is exactly what we have done—we have adopted the UN flag and the UN constitution (charter). This very thing has at once limited our sovereignty and independence as a nation, the very thing our prophet-leaders have warned against.[18]

---

[18]   Ezra Taft Benson said, "the U.N.'s potential for evil far outweighs its potential for good" (*An Enemy Hath Done This*, p. 202). He also warned: "We should get out of the U.N. and get the U.N. out of the United States" (Ibid., p. 208).

Part III:
PERSPECTIVES ON AMERICA'S FUTURE

The true destiny of America is religious, not political;
it is spiritual, not physical.

—Alvin R. Dyer

8
Communism
in the Last Days

And those who do not believe in God
talk of socialism or anarchism,
of the transformation of all humanity
on a new pattern, so that it all comes to the same:
they're the same questions turned inside out.

—Fyoder Dostoevsky

Communism
and the present course
of the Western nations
will eventually bring us
to slavery, despair, and destruction,
the inevitable end of every person, nation,
and civilization which persists in refusing
to seek the guidance of the Holy Spirit.

—Marion G. Romney

In 1989 the Berlin Wall came tumbling down in loud protest for freedom. This was followed by the collapse of communism in the Ukraine in 1991, when Soviet Russia gained liberating freedoms never felt before under the dictatorship of communist rule. It was a new beginning, a new chapter for history books, another saga in man's quest for his inalienable right to freedom: freedom to think, act, live, and worship according to his conscience. As the oft repeated phrase is rehearsed, 'history repeats itself,' so it had in the Eastern Bloc countries of communist Europe. For at other times in history's long past, when coercion was the dictator's arm, people would live only so long under the oppressed government. Then it became this motto: "Give me liberty or give me death!" And ultimately whether by death or liberation freedom prevailed.[1]

Is Communism Dead?

Since the remarkable revolutionary happenings over the past decade other countries have followed in pursuit of their right to democracy. This is only as it should be. The dilemma is that apathy follows such conquest. People now have the mistaken notion that communism is dead. 'The Cold War is over,' they surmise, 'and so is communist fear.' Yet with all the remarkable advancements for a democratic world, communism is yet alive, albeit well hidden from society's norm. As one publication observed:

> The spread of democracy has by no means eradicated political repression or conflict.... In the last several years...what enthusiasts

---

[1]   "Men will be free! I have hoped for twenty years that the Russian system would break up. There is no freedom under it, and sooner or later the people will rise against it. They cannot oppress those fundamentals of civilization and of God. They cannot crush their people always. Men will be free!" (Ezra Taft Benson as quoted in Duane S. Crowther, *Prophecy: Key to the Future*, p. 12)

at the start of the decade were calling 'the worldwide democratic revolution,' has cooled considerably. The headlines announcing that country after country was shrugging off dictatorial rule and embarking on a democratic path have given way to an intermittent but rising stream of troubling reports....[2]

Another author has said that we suffer from "Perhaps the greatest ruse that has ever been foisted upon an educated society." It is the "oft repeated declaration that 'COMMUNISM IS DEAD.' "[3]

While it is true that the Cold War is a thing of the past and that the imminent threat of a communist takeover is not anticipated, it is also true that communism is *not* dead. Its principles still thrive in many aspects of world politics, even in parts of American government. It is this author's belief, substantiated by prophetic statements, that communism will yet play crucial roles in the last days' scenario.

The scriptures, especially that book which was written for our day, the Book of Mormon, repeatedly affirm that a secret worldwide combination would rise in the latter-days, and with its rising seduce the nations of the globe to join alliances with it. For instance, Nephi said: "Behold, I prophecy concerning the last days...there [will be] secret combinations, even as in times of old, according to the combinations of the devil, for he is the founder of all these things; yea, the founder of murder, and works of darkness; yea, and he leadeth them by the neck with a flaxen cord, until he bindeth them with his strong cords forever" (2 Nephi 26:14, 22). And Moroni, warning the Gentiles of the last days, has written: "Wherefore, the Lord commandeth you, when ye shall see these things come among

---

2   *Foreign Affairs* Jan/Feb 1997, p. 85. The Sep/Oct 1997 issue of *Foreign Affairs* says, the "democratic hegemony is a mere flash in the long vistas of recorded history. One wonders how deeply democracy has sunk roots in the previously non-democratic countries in the years since the collapse of the totalitarian challenges" (pp. 4-5).

3   David M. Balmforth, *America's Coming Crisis: Prophetic Warnings, Divine Destiny*, p. 155; hereafter cited as *America's Coming Crisis.*

you that ye shall awake to a sense of your awful situation, because of this secret combination which shall be among you; or woe be unto it, because of the blood of them who have been slain; for they cry from the dust for vengeance upon it, and also upon those who built it up. For it cometh to pass that whoso buildeth it up seeketh to overthrow the freedom of all lands, nations, and countries; and it bringeth to pass the destruction of all people..." (Ether 8:24-25 [22-26]).

Elder Ezra Taft Benson said: "The world-wide secret conspiracy which has risen up in our day to fulfill these prophecies is easily identified."[4] And Elder Bruce R. McConkie, writing on the same theme, has said:

> Moroni turns the key so that all who have ears to hear can understand what the secret combination is and can identify those who build it up. "For it cometh to pass," he says, "that whoso buildeth it up seeketh to overthrow the freedom of all lands, nations, and countries." *This is a worldwide conspiracy.* It is now entrenched in many nations, and it seeks dominion over *all* nations. It is Godless, atheistic, and operates by compulsion. *It is communism.* "And it bringeth to pass the destruction of all people, for it is built up by the devil, who is the father of all lies; even that same liar who beguiled our first parents, yea, even that same liar who hath caused man to commit murder from the beginning; who hath hardened the hearts of men that they have murdered the prophets, and stoned them, and cast them out from the beginning."[5]

Book of Mormon prophets are not the only figures of antiquity that warned of a world conspiracy in the last days. John the Revelator, for

---

4   As quoted in Duane S. Crowther, *Prophecy—Key to the Future,* p. 12.
5   *The Millennial Messiah,* p. 66; emphasis added.

example, symbolically wrote that he saw a "woman sit upon a scarlet coloured beast, full of names of blasphemy…and the woman was arrayed in purple and scarlet colour, and decked with gold and precious stones and pearls, having a golden cup in her hand full of abominations and filthiness of her fornication: And upon her forehead was a name written, MYSTERY, BABYLON THE GREAT, THE MOTHER OF HARLOTS AND ABOMINATIONS OF THE EARTH" (Revelation 17:3-5). Although these versus by John could contain multiple meanings, putting the scriptures into perspective with the forces of modern times there is no doubt that one of the meanings is present day communism. This would include the initial organization of the United Nations, American socialism, and corrupt government of any sort.

Socialism, Forerunner to Communism

President Marion G. Romney said: "We here in the United States, in converting our government into a welfare state, have ourselves adopted much of socialism."[6] And President Ezra Taft Benson taught that "Communism is essentially socialism."[7]

Politics, economics, and education all play a part of the socialist reform. It is the age-old question of how much government should be allowed into private businesses and personal lives. During the Cold War era the Communists obliged to have said they had "hundreds [of communists] in our [American] governmental offices."[8] Is it any different today, even with the demise of the Cold War? Are there not politicians and policies that disturb our sovereign way of life? President David O. McKay said: "Under

---

6   As quoted in H. Verlan Andersen, *The Great and Abominable Church of the Devil*, p. 94.
7   *This Nation Shall Endure*, p. 90.
8   *Prophets, Principles and National Survival*, p. 221; hereafter cited as *PPNS*.

communism you lose your liberties immediately and perhaps your life. Under Socialism, you lose your liberties a little more slowly but just as surely."[9] And Ezra Taft Benson said, "The prophets in our day have continually warned...that our greatest threat from Socialistic Communism lies within our country..."[10] As long as socialism survives so does communism.

Socialism, Communism, Humanism—all Atheism![11]

In his classic novel, *The Brothers Karamazov*, Fyoder Dostoevsky has one character say: "socialism is not merely the labour question, it is before all things the atheistic question, the question of the form taken by atheism to-day, the question of the tower of Babel built without God, not to mount to heaven from earth but to set up heaven on earth."

Just as the Constitution of the United States and the initial American government was founded on a belief in God, so Marx's *Manifesto* and the communist empire was built on atheistic tenets. A modern prophet of the true and living God warned: "Do not let advocates of communism mislead you in their attempt to denounce capitalism. Fundamental in the belief and promulgation of communism is the denial of the existence of God.... At heart communism is atheistic, and fascism is equally antagonistic to freedom and to other Christian principles—even denying the divinity of Jesus Christ and the existence of God."[12] Another apostle of the Church warned: "May I assure you that communism is not merely an economic program. It is a total philosophy of life, atheistic and utterly opposed to

---

9   *Man May Know for Himself,* p. 356.
10   As quoted in Duane S. Crowther, *Prophecy—Key to the Future,* p. 11.
11   "Today there are in this country enemies in the form of 'isms,' " said President David O. McKay. "I call them anti-Americanisms" (*Gospel Ideals,* p. 304).
12   David O. McKay, as quoted in *PPNS,* p. 217.

all we hold dear as a great Christian nation."[13] And Elder Hugh B. Brown said of communist threat:

> The threat of communism is sinister, and its dangers are immi-
> nent. Hundreds of millions of our fellow beings are being relent-
> lessly imbued with the satanic ideology that the Father-hood of
> God, the Saviorhood of Christ, and the brotherhood of man are
> stupid myths, that religion is nothing but a tranquilizing opiate.
> They seek to deprive men of physical, mental, and spiritual freedom
> while endowing the state with monstrous supremacy. This relentless
> indoctrination is but a continuation of the war that began when
> Satan's plan of force was rejected by the Father.[14]

One communist leader exemplified the satanic doctrine of communism by saying: "We must hate Christians and Christianity. Even the best of them must be considered our worst enemies. Christian love is an obstacle to the development of the revolution. Down with love of one's neighbor! What we want is hate. Only then will we conquer the universe."[15]

It's Not Over Yet

Soon after the Cold War ended and while the Western world was still celebrating the birth of a new era, Russian leader Mikhail Gorbachev soothed his country against the idea that communism was dead. Gorbachev said:

---

13 Ezra Taft Benson, *So Shall Ye Reap*, p. 163.
14 *CR* April 1963, p. 7.
15 *PPNS*, p. 217.

Gentleman, comrades, do not be concerned about all you hear about glasnost and perestroika and democracy in the coming years. These are primarily for outward consumption. *There will be no significant internal change within the Soviet Union, other than for cosmetic purposes....* Our purpose is to disarm the Americans and to *let them fall asleep.*[16]

The threat of a communist takeover is not prevalent to the general populace today. We don't hear about communist regimes like we did during the long-standing Cold War. But to conclude that communism is dead is a heady assumption, an assumption which attests that perhaps we are fallen asleep. Contrary to popular belief, communism is still alive in Russia. It is active in China. Communist principles abound in the strategic plans of the United Nations,[17] and socialism—forerunner to communism—is active in many aspects of American government. Ezra Taft Benson said of this:

---

[16] As quoted in *America's Coming Crisis*, p. 132; emphasis added. As 1999 drew to a close, Russian President Boris Yeltstin threatened the United States by saying, "...Russia is a great power that possesses a nuclear arsenal.... It is us who will dictate" (The Associated Press, "Yelstin Blasts Clinton, Touts Nuclear Arsenal," *The Salt Lake Tribune*, Friday December 10, 1999, A-19).

[17] "When one stops to consider the degree of communist influence at the U.N....it is no wonder that the U.N. has never performed a real anti-communist act.... On the other hand, it has helped the forces of communism on many occasions" (*An Enemy Hath Done This*, p. 207).

While we might effectively bridle or destroy every so-called communist within our own borders, we shall not vanquish this political virus, and its common forerunner, state socialism, so long as people are determined to achieve security through state-imposed materialistic schemes rather than through righteous living and wholesome activity as free men.[18]

And Elder Marion G. Romney said, "notwithstanding my abhorrence of it, I am persuaded that socialism is the wave of the present and of the foreseeable future."[19] Thus, what the prophets have warned about communism in the last days is not something of the past; it is not all said and done with. As long as American socialism persists then so does the threat of communism, for socialism *is* its forerunner.

---

[18] *So Shall Ye Reap*, p. 163.

[19] As quoted in *The Great and Abominable Church of the Devil*, p. 95.

9
The Lord's Government

*The government of the Almighty has always
been very dissimilar to the governments of men,
whether we refer to His religious government,
or to the government of nations.
The government of God has always tended to promote
peace, unity, harmony, strength, and happiness;
while that of man has been productive of
confusion, disorder, weakness, and misery.*

—Joseph Smith

*For unto us a child is born,
unto us a son is given;
and the government shall be upon his shoulder;
and his name shall be called Wonderful, Counselor,
The Mighty God,
The Everlasting Father,
The Prince of Peace.*

Of the increase of government and peace there is no end...

Isaiah 9: 6-7; 2 Nephi 19:6-7

The Early Church and It's Falling Away

After His resurrection and before His ascension into the heavens thereafter, the Savior commissioned His apostles with this charge: "Go ye therefore, and teach all nations, baptizing them in the name of the Father, and of the Son, and of the Holy Ghost. Teaching them to observe all things whatsoever I have commanded you." With this charge the apostles also received a promise: "I am with you alway," said the Savior, "even unto the end of the world" (Matthew 27:19-20). The authority to perform miracles and the saving ordinances of the gospel, such as baptism and the confirmation of the Holy Ghost, had already been given to the Twelve (see Matthew 10:1), but now they had the complete directive of preaching the gospel to the world.

The Savior's Church is one "built upon the foundation of the apostles and prophets, Jesus Christ himself being the chief corner stone" (Ephesians 2:20). In order for the Quorum of Twelve to have functioned in its fully orchestrated capacity, the vacancy in the quorum, caused by the apostasy and suicide of Judas Iscariot, had to be filled. This was accomplished by the calling of Matthias (see Acts 1:21-26). Thus again fully organized as Christ had intended, the Twelve were ready to fulfill their commission and carry the "good news" to all inhabitants of the earth, teaching Christ and raising the warning voice. Many heard the warning voice for what it was and gladly accepted baptism. Others heard what they termed to be "fanatics," and chose, to their own determent and peril, not to believe. Still others not content to ignore the Lord's anointed, felt driven to "kick against the pricks," and thus, the persecution and martyrdom of the apostles.

When the last apostle fell dead the priesthood that Christ had given to His earthly church also died. No longer did the fledgling Church receive direct revelation as the apostles had received. The members were left to their own guesswork. It became a time of confusion, a time when many churches evolved, each interpreting the scriptures and doctrines to their own liking, each professing a "form of godliness" but denying the power thereof" (see Joseph Smith—History 1:19; see also Isaiah 29:13). The world plummeted into the dark ages or, doctrinally speaking, the Great Apostasy.

The Great Apostasy Foretold

Many ancient prophets warned that a great apostasy would occur. The prophet Amos, for example, had warned: "Behold, the days come, saith the Lord God, that I will send a famine in the land, not a famine of bread, nor a thirst for water, but of hearing the words of the Lord. And they shall wander from sea to sea, and from the north even to the east, they shall run to and fro to seek the word of the Lord, and they shall not find it" (Amos 8:11-12). Paul, one of the apostles of the early church, warned that there would "come a falling away" (see 2 Thessalonians 2:1-3). The Savior Himself warned of the apostasy that would occur. To His apostles He said, "many shall come in my name, saying, I am Christ [I am the true church]; and shall deceive many" (Matthew 24:5). "For there shall arise false Christs, and false prophets [and false churches], and shall shew great signs and wonders; insomuch that, if it were possible, they shall deceive the very elect" (Matthew 24:24).

It is a fact all too apparent both in scripture and in secular history that a "falling away" or great apostasy from the early church did occur; and "behold, the darkness [did] cover the earth, and gross darkness the minds of the people." But thankfully the prophecies stretched beyond the apostasy; the dark ages were not to last: "but the Lord shall arise upon thee, and his glory shall be seen upon thee" (Isaiah 60:2).

A Restoration Foretold

Just as many prophets foretold of the Great Apostasy, so also was the day of restoration foretold by many ancient prophets. For instance, the

Lord had told Isaiah of that day, saying: "Forasmuch as this people draw near me with their mouth, and with their lips do honor me, but have removed their heart far from me, and their fear toward me is taught by the precept of men: Therefore, behold, I will proceed to do a marvelous work among this people, even a marvelous work and a wonder: for the wisdom of their wise men shall perish, and the understanding of their prudent men shall be hid" (Isaiah 29:13-14). This same poet-prophet also recorded: "And it shall come to pass in that day, that the Lord shall set his hand again *the second time* to recover the remnant of his people... *And he shall set up an ensign for the nations*, and shall assemble the outcasts of Israel, and gather together the dispersed of Judah from the four corners of the Earth" (Isaiah 11:11-12). "Moreover," said the Lord to Ezekiel, "I will make a covenant of peace with them; it shall be an everlasting covenant with them: and I will place them, and multiply them, and will set my sanctuary in the midst of them for evermore" (Ezekiel 37:26). Of the Lord's sanctuary, Isaiah tells us that "it shall come to pass in the last days, the mountain of the LORD's house shall be established in the top of the mountains, and shall be exalted above the hills; and all nations shall flow unto it" (Isaiah 2:2).[1]

A Marvelous Theophany!

The long night of apostasy that set on the world when the last apostle was martyred had by 1820 begun to be dispersed. It began when a young boy, fourteen and one-half years of age and by the common name of Joseph Smith, entered a grove of trees in upstate New York and asked God in prayer the question of the ages: "Which of all the churches is right, and which should I join?" This was a solemn question asked by many of his time—a time that consisted of numerous revivals by myriad churches to

---

[1]   *Utah*, from the Ute Indians, literally means *top of the mountains*.

reclaim the sinner. But it was Joseph Smith who took the question seriously and then took it to God. James' directive to "ask of God" (James 1:5) was no doubt appealing to the young man; the passage no doubt helped lead him to the experience in the grove. In his own words, Joseph said of the Epistle of James: "Never did any passage of scripture come with more power to the heart of man than this did at this time to mine" (Joseph Smith—History 1:12). Pondering the scriptural counsel of James, young Joseph believed he could ask God the question of his mind and that God would *not* upbraid him.[2]

In making his attempt to "ask of God" Joseph kneeled in a secluded grove near his parents' farm in Palmyra, New York. Joseph, with faith like the ancients—faith like that of a child—didn't know *how* he'd be answered; he only believed he *would* be answered. The answer came in a "pillar of light," recorded Joseph, which hung "exactly over my head…. When the light rested upon me I saw *two Personages,* whose brightness and glory defy all description, standing above me in the air."

Not one divine personage, but two! The Father *and* the Son!

Down with the Nicene Creed that proposed God was some ephemeral being, filling the immensity of space yet was nowhere in particular; that said the Father, Son, and Holy Ghost were one intangible God without body, parts, or passion!

Down with the philosophies of man which say that God is dead, that revelation is no more, that the cannon of scripture is filled!

Down with the dark ages and the great apostasy! Joseph saw two personages—a marvelous Theophany! "and they did in reality speak to me," was his solemn testimony that had, like the apostles of old, cost him his life in 1844.

While the world went on its merry way, while the churches of Palmyra and the surrounding states held their revivals, the enacted drama of the restoration had begun in a quiet grove of trees. Yet the revelation that opened

---

2   *Scold* or *criticize.*

to Joseph that spring morning was just the beginning. A consecutive stream of revelations and visions were soon to follow, including keys of authority that had to be restored. This was the dispensation of the fullness of times, when all the principles and ordinances and keys of authority pertaining to the everlasting gospel were to be restored to the earth in their fullness.

"A Stone Cut out of the Mountain without Hands"

In the Book of Daniel we read that King Nebuchadnezzar had a dream that contained weird images and symbolic meaning. Troubled by his dream, the King sent for interpreters and promised them that if they gave him the "interpretation thereof," he would give them "gifts and rewards and great honour" (Daniel 2:6). But alas, no one could interpret Nebuchadnezzar's dream. That is until Daniel came to the King and said: "The secret which the king hath demanded cannot the wise men, the astrologers, the magicians, the soothsayers, shew unto the king; But there is a God in heaven that revealeth secrets, and maketh known to the king Nebuchadnezzar what shall be in the latter days. Thy dream, and the visions of thy head upon thy bed, are these" (Daniel 2:27-28). Then Daniel interpreted Nebuchadnezzar's dream, which is this:

> Thou, O king, sawest, and beheld a great image. This great image, whose brightness was excellent, stood before thee; and the form thereof was terrible.
> This image's head was of fine gold, his breast and his arms of silver, his belly and his thighs of brass,
> His legs of iron, his feet part of iron and part of clay.

> Thou sawest till that a stone was cut out without hands, which smote the image upon his feet that were of iron and clay, and brake them in pieces.
>
> Then was the iron, the clay, the brass, the silver, and the gold, broken to pieces together, and became like the chaff of the summer threshingfloors; and the wind carried them away, that no place was found for them: and the stone that smote the image became a great mountain, and filled the whole earth (Daniel 2:31-35).

The terrible image that took center stage in the king's dream was symbolic of the kingdoms of the world. Some were symbolized as clay, some of brass, some of silver, and still others of gold. Continuing his own explanation of Nebuchadnezzar's dream, Daniel said:

> Thou, O king, art a king of kings: for the God of heaven hath given thee a kingdom, power, and strength, and glory....
>
> And after thee shall arise another kingdom inferior to thee, and another third kingdom of brass, which shall bear rule over all the earth.
>
> And the fourth kingdom shall be strong as iron: forasmuch as iron breaketh in pieces and subdueth all things: and as iron that breaketh all these, shall it brake in pieces and bruise.
>
> And whereas thou sawest the feet and toes, part of potters' clay, and part of iron, the kingdom shall be divided: but there shall be in it of the strength of iron, forasmuch as thou sawest the iron mixed with miry clay.
>
> And as the toes of the feet were part of iron, and part of clay, so the kingdom shall be partly strong, and partly broken.
>
> And whereas thou sawest iron mixed with miry clay, they shall mingle themselves with the seed of men: but they shall not cleave one to another, even as iron is not mixed with clay (Daniel 2:36-43).

Although Daniel's interpretation can be difficult to understand if one is not familiar with the empires of the past and of scriptural symbolism, there is useful commentary from numerous church leaders. From Apostle Parley P. Pratt's book titled *Voice of Warning*, we have this:

> Babylon, the most ancient and renowned city of the world, was pleasantly situated on the banks of a majestic river that flowed through the plains of Shinar, near to which the tower of Babel once stood. It was laid out four-square, and surrounded with a wall upwards of three hundred feet high, and sixty miles in circumference; having a hundred gates of *brass*, with bars of *iron*; twenty-five gates on each side, which opened to streets running through the city a distance of fifteen miles; thus forming the whole city into exact squares of equal size. In the midst of these squares were beautiful gardens, adorned with trees and walks, diversified with flowers of varied hue; while the houses were built upon the borders of the squares, directly fronting the streets. In the midst of this city sat Nebuchadnezzar, enthroned in royal splendour and magnificence, and swaying his sceptre over all the kingdoms of the world, when it pleased God, in a vision of the night, to unveil the dark curtain of the future, and to present before him, at one view, the history of the world, even down to the consummation of all things...
>
> In this great view of the subject we have presented before us [the interpretation of Nebuchadnezzar's dream], in succession [we have], first, the kingdom of Nebuchadnezzar; second, the Medes and Persians, who took Babylon from Belshazzar, and reigned over all the earth; third, the Greeks, under Alexander, who conquered the world, and reigned in the midst of Babylon; and fourth, the Roman empire, which subdued all things; fifth, its division into eastern and western empires, and its final breaking

up or subdivision into the various kingdoms of modern Europe, represented by the feet and toes, part of iron and part of clay.[3]

"And in the days of these kings," explained Daniel, "shall the God of heaven set up a kingdom, which shall never be destroyed: and the kingdom shall not be left to other people, but it shall break in pieces and consume all these kingdoms, and it shall stand for ever. Forasmuch as thou sawest that the stone was cut out of the mountain without hands, and that it brake in pieces the iron, the brass, the clay, the silver, and the gold; the great God hath made known to the king what shall come to pass hereafter: and the dream is certain, and the interpretation thereof sure" (Daniel 2:44-45). This is the subject to which this lengthy treatise has finally taken us. Concerning this kingdom, this "stone cut out of the mountain without hands," Elder Pratt said: "Suffice it to say, that the kingdom spoken of by Daniel is something to be organized in the last days by the God of heaven Himself, without the aid of human institutions or the precepts of men."[4]

The kingdom to which Daniel referred *is* the Restoration Church, even The Church of Jesus Christ of Latter-day Saints, cut as if out of a mountain without the hand of man; cut by the hand of God and of His revelation. It is the Restoration Kingdom that is gaining momentum in the world and which will eventually consume, and in a not-too-distant day, "brake in pieces all these other kingdoms." All people shall then be subject to the theocratic rule of the Lord's government. Such is the Kingdom of God on earth.

---

3   *Voice of Warning*, pp. 11-12, 14.
4   Ibid. p. 16.

The Lord's Government as now Established

The Lord's Government as now established is where the fullness of the gospel is had, and where the proper principles and ordinances of the gospel are both taught and performed; it is where priesthood authority exists to perform such ordinances and teach such principles. It is where temples are erected and where saving ordinances for both the living and the dead are performed. The Lord's government as now established is where true prophets are found, where revelation flourishes, where the cannon of scripture is yet open, and where the people have taken upon themselves the name of Christ.

Joseph Smith taught, "...where there is a priest of God—a minister who has power and authority from God to administer in the ordinances of the gospel and officiate in the priesthood of God—there is the kingdom of God."[5] He also warned of the "judgments of God [which] have rested upon people, cities, and nations" in time's past "in consequence of rejecting the Gospel of Jesus Christ and the Prophets whom God hath sent" among them. Such "was the case with the cities of Sodom and Gomorrah, that were destroyed for rejecting the Prophets."[6]

The Lord's Government—the Kingdom of God—as established in our day is The Church of Jesus Christ of Latter-day Saints. Of the Restoration Church, President Wilford Woodruff said in 1872:

> The kingdom is established, the work of God is manifest in the earth, the Saints have come up here into the valleys of the mountains, and they are erecting the house of God in the tops thereof, for the nations to flow unto [see Isaiah 2:2]. A standard of truth has been lifted up to the people, and from the commencement of this work the Latter-day Saints have been fulfilling that flood of

---

5   *TPJS*, p. 271.
6   Ibid.

revelation and prophecy which was given formerly concerning this great work in the last days. I rejoice in this, and also because we have every reason to expect a continuation of these blessings unto Zion.[7]

President Joseph Fielding Smith said that "the kingdom of God is the Church of Jesus Christ, and it is the kingdom that shall endure forever."[8] Concerning the position the Church will hold in world affairs, President John Taylor boldly testified in 1853:

> Let us now notice our political position in the world. What are we going to do? We are going to possess the earth. Why? Because it belongs to Jesus Christ, and he belongs to us, and we to him. We are all one, and will take the kingdom and possess it under the whole heavens, and reign over it for ever and ever. Now, ye kings and emperors, help yourselves, if you can. This is the truth, and it may as well be told at this time as at any other.[9]

The Lord's Government as Established during the Millennium

It should be noted here that the current position of the Church with regard to political matters is strictly in line with the Constitution. We firmly believe in the separating powers of church and state. It is the kingdom of God in the millennial day that will rule the world with political sanction. It will be a theocracy, Christ as our Governor: "And he shall judge among the nations, and shall rebuke many people: and they shall

---

[7]   *The Discourses of Wilford Woodruff,* p. 184.
[8]   *Doctrines of Salvation,* p. 230.
[9]   *The Gospel Kingdom,* p. 312.

beat their swords into plowshares, and their spears into pruninghooks: nation shall not lift up sword against nation, neither shall they learn war any more.... for out of Zion shall go forth the law, and the word of the Lord from Jerusalem" (Isaiah 2:3-4).

How the Church will gain such momentum in world affairs and become the theocratic government of the world is explained through the prophecy of Nebuchadnezzar's dream as interpreted by the prophet Daniel and as has already been discussed. Using the words of President Joseph Fielding Smith, "*When Christ comes, the political kingdom will be given to the Church.* The Lord is going to make an end to all nations; that means this nation as well as any other. *The kingdom of God is the Church*, but during the millennium, the multitudes upon the face of the earth who are not in the Church will have to be governed, and many of their officers, who will be elected, may not be members of the Church."[10] President Smith also explained: "When the Savior prayed, 'Thy kingdom come,' he had reference to the kingdom in heaven which is to come when the millennial reign starts."[11] Of this the scripture says: "Call upon the Lord, that his kingdom [Church] may go forth upon the earth, that the inhabitants thereof may receive it, and be prepared for the days to come, in the which the Son of Man shall come down in heaven, clothed in the brightness of his glory, to meet the kingdom of God which is set up on the earth. Wherefore, may the kingdom of God go forth, that the kingdom of heaven may come, that thou, O God, mayest be glorified in heaven so on earth, that thine enemies may be subdued; for thine is the honor, power and glory, forever and ever. Amen" (D&C 65:5-6).

---

10   *Doctrines of Salvation*, p. 230.
11   Ibid.

It appears that the "kingdom in heaven" and the "kingdom of God which is set up on the earth" (The Church of Jesus Christ of Latter-day Saints) will unite and thus become a theocratic government that will rule the world. Thus the millennial kingdom as will be established will be a combination of the present day Church organization and the kingdom of heaven that will come with Christ. Included in this eventual makeup of the kingdom will be Enoch's City of Zion and the future New Jerusalem. Righteousness and peace will reign and the great day of millennial rest and renewal will have begun. Such is the destiny of The Church of Jesus Christ of Latter-day Saints, the kingdom of God on earth. Such is the destiny of the affairs and the politics of this world: they shall all crumble and fall before the majestic throne of Him whose right it is to reign.

The fulfillment of these prophecies begun in a secluded burrow of trees in upstate New York in 1820, when a boy possessing the most common of names, Joseph Smith, saw into eternity and changed the history of the world. The restoration is indeed one of the great pillars of eternity!

10
America and the Second Coming

The Millennium
is dawning upon the world,
we are at the end of the six thousand years,
and the great day of rest,
the Millennium of which the Lord has spoken,
will soon dawn,
and the Savior will come
in the clouds of heaven
to reign over his people
on the earth one thousand years.

—Wilford Woodruff

The twenty-first century is upon us—a new millennium! Where will it take us?

I have given it as my decided opinion that if another book is to be written on the Second Coming it should be written by a duly authorized representative of the Church, poignantly from one of its apostolic leaders. I do not attempt to reconcile my opinion here. However, if we are to see

America in true perspective, we must know something of the last days and its prophetic promises, as well as its warnings. We must understand what role the United States, and more precisely the land of America, is to play in the approaching drama. Whereas the millennial kingdom has been discussed in chapter 9, chapter 10 is devoted to "the last days," the time just prior to the great millennium—the times in which we now live. Hopefully this will help us better prepare for the trying times ahead. (Note: this chapter is not arranged in chronological order of events but only *as events* that are to transpire.)

Earth's Temporal Timeline

We know not how long our first parents, Adam and Eve, lived in the Garden of Eden; we only know they lived there as innocents, and after the fall were driven from their paradise into the lone and dreary world. The Prophet Joseph Smith proposed that four thousand years elapsed from the time Adam was driven from the Garden until the coming of Christ in time's meridian. Two thousand years has since past from the coming of Christ until now. Thus, a total of six thousand years has passed since Adam and Eve walked out of the Garden as fallen mortals.

While banished to the Isle of Patmos (see Revelation 1:1-2) the apostle John, also known as the "disciple whom Jesus loved" (see John 20:2; 21:7; 21:20), received and recorded grand revelations regarding the earth's temporal lifeline. John saw the vision piece-meal at a time. The earth's lifeline was to include seven thousand years of existence, the seventh being the Sabbatical or millennial era when it would be renewed and again receive its paradisiacal glory. John describes the individual time periods as "seals" (see Revelation 6:3, 5, 7, 9, 12; 8:1). It is a fact attested to by many prophets, as well as events, that we are now living in the latter period of the sixth seal, a time just prior to the Millennium. Elder Bruce R. McConkie emphasized this fact when he wrote:

We are now living during the final years of the sixth seal, that thousand year period which began in 1000 A.D. and will continue through the Saturday night of time and until just before the Sabbatical era when Christ shall reign personally on earth, when all of the blessings of the Great Millennium shall be poured out upon this planet. This, accordingly, is the era when the signs of the times shall be shown forth, and they are in fact everywhere to be seen.[1]

Although John saw the drama to be acted out in each individual seal, the Revelator gave more emphasis to the sixth and seventh seals than any other seal. The reason for such emphasis is readily apparent since these periods would contain the most dramatic consequences. Some of the consequences no doubt will be warfare, disease, pollution, earthquakes, famine and other natural disasters, a reeling to and fro of the earth and other planetary systems, great signs and wonders both in the heavens and in the earth. All such things are given as *signs* that the hour approaches when the Bridegroom will come to meet His bride (the Church) and receive her unto Himself. In his day, President Spencer W. Kimball testified:

> Just as surely as Jesus was born in Bethlehem, just so surely will he come again, a resurrected, glorified being, and with him will come hosts, and there will be many spectacular changes. It will not be the end of the world in the sense of annihilation, but the end of its present relationships, and there will be many, many changes. Beginning with the bridegroom's coming will come the celestializing of this earth and tremendous changes which we can hardly think of or believe...[2]

---

1 *Doctrinal New Testament Commentary III*, pp. 485-486.
2 *TSWK*, pp. 440-441.

America and the Trying Times of the Last Days

The topic of the last days is strikingly difficult for some people. There are no great mysteries as to the reason why this is so, for the last days are ones of great trial and tribulation. This is explicit in Elder Bruce R. McConkie's General Conference address concerning the last days, as given in April 1979. In part, Elder McConkie said:

> ...Peace has been taken from the earth, the angels of destruction have begun their work, and their swords shall not be sheathed until the Prince of Peace comes to destroy the wicked and usher in the great Millennium.... There will be wars in one nation and kingdom after another until war is poured out upon all nations and two hundred million men of war mass their armaments at Armageddon.... Bands of Gadianton robbers will infest every nation, immorality and murder and crime will increase, and it will seem as though every man's hand is against his brother.[3]

At the next Spring General Conference, just one year later, Elder McConkie took the same theme as before and warned that the greatest trials are yet to come. His address is replete with urgency:

> We shall yet face greater perils, we shall yet be tested with more severe trials, and we shall yet weep more tears of sorrow than we have ever known before.... We tremble because of the sorrows and wars and plagues that shall cover the earth. We weep for those in the true Church who are weak and wayward and worldly and who

---

3   As quoted in *Spiritual Survival in the Last Days*, pp. 49-50.

fall by the wayside as the caravan of the kingdom rolls forward.... All that is yet to be shall go forward in the midst of greater evils and perils and desolations than have been known on earth at any time.... Amid tears of sorrow—our hearts heavy with foreboding— we see evil and crime and carnality covering the earth. Liars and thieves and adulterers and homosexuals and murderers scarcely seek to hide their abominations from our view. Iniquity abounds. There is no peace on earth. We see evil forces everywhere uniting to destroy the family, to ridicule morality and decency, to glorify all that is lewd and base. We see wars and plagues and pestilence. Nations rise and fall. Blood and carnage and death are everywhere. Gadianton robbers fill the judgement seats in many nations. An evil power seeks to overthrow the freedom of all nations and countries. Satan reigns in the hearts of men; it is the great day of his power.[4]

Truly such chaotic structure would seem overwhelming, even verging on the incomprehensible, if only read about in books and conference addresses. But the truth is, such overwhelming odds are at the present doors. Suffice it to be said they are knocking loudly. The signs of the Lord's coming are everywhere to be seen.

Prophecy warns that times are to get worse before they get better. America will yet see an overflowing scourge, as disease and disaster, famine and bloodshed will reign on this continent, and the hearts of men will fail them. Our patriotic values will continue to be assaulted, and the Constitution of the United States will be in peril. Communism will again stretch its influence abroad, and governments will fail as immorality and

---

4   Ibid. p. 50.

crime will continue to plague society. Earthquakes and tempests and the calamities of nature will reek havoc to our nation, and the United States will again be plummeted to the battle ranks of another world war.[5]

America's Destiny and Triumph Amid Times of Chaos

America has yet to pass through a refiner's fire before its ultimate time of rest and renewal. But through such "heat" of the last days America will triumph. That truth has already been decreed in sacred writ. For instance, concerning the perilous times the Constitution will face, Elder Melvin J. Ballard said: "It is true that our Prophet saw the very Constitution hang as by a thread, *but thank the Lord he never saw the thread break, and it shall not break.*"[6] President Brigham Young asked the question: "Will the Constitution be destroyed?" Then President Young answered, "No, it will

---

5   President George Albert Smith said: "I fear that the time is coming...unless we can call the people of this world to repent of their ways, the great war that has just passed [World War II] will be an insignificant thing, as far as calamity is concerned, compared to that which is before us" (as quoted *Spiritual Survival in the Last Days*, p. 31). In his day, President David O. McKay warned: "Approximately only a quarter of a century ago, the world listened to the clanging of arms of nations fighting in a world-wide war that was supposed to end war forever. Up to that time it was the bloodiest war in history. Again, misguided leaders of nations, worshipping the god of materialism, have brought on World War II, and unless the nations avoid the evil things which caused this war, there will be a World War III even more destructive, more terrible than the present murderous conflict. Like causes produce like effects" (*Gospel Ideals*, p. 278). And from Elder Bruce R. McConkie we have this: "It may be, for instance, that nothing except the power of faith and the authority of the priesthood can save individuals and congregations from the *atomic holocausts that surely shall be*" (as quoted in *Spiritual Survival in the Last Days*, p. 53; emphasis added).

6   *Sermons and Missionary Services of Melvin J. Ballard*, p. 271; emphasis added.

be held inviolate by this [the Latter-day Saint] people; and, as Joseph Smith said: 'The time will come when the destiny of the nation will hang upon a single thread. At that critical juncture, this people will step forth and save it from the threatened destruction.' It will be so."[7]

It appears that when the Constitution hangs in the balance the latter-day saints will stand ready to preserve it. They will allow its burning light of liberty to be raised in the City of Zion where all of the Constitutional principles of freedom will be upheld to the world.

If we comprehend in true perspective the ultimate destiny the American nation has before it, then we must know that anarchy will abound as the love of men waxes cold. But we will also know that a celestial crown awaits our America, for when Christ comes again the Stars and Stripes will be flying in the breeze over the valiant living testaments of Christ—the latter-day saints and other honorable people. President Brigham Young taught: "When the day comes in which the Kingdom of God will bear rule, the flag of the United States will proudly flutter unsullied on the flagstaff of liberty and equal rights, without a spot to sully its fair surface; the glorious flag our fathers have bequeathed to us will then be unfurled to the breeze by those who have power to hoist it aloft and defend its sanctity."[8] And President Ezra Taft Benson said: "It may…cost us blood before we are through. It is my conviction, however, that when the Lord comes, the Stars and Stripes will be floating on the breeze over this people."[9]

> *Oh say, does that star spangled banner yet wave—*
> *O'er the land of the free*
> *and the home of the brave?*[10]

---

[7]   *JD* 7:15

[8]   *DBY* p. 360.

[9]   *Banner*, p. 33.

[10]   The Star Spangled Banner. *Hymns of The Church of Jesus Christ of Latter-day Saints*, #340.

Nations No More and the Return of Pangaea

On Christmas day 1832 the Prophet Joseph Smith received a revelation concerning the last days and "the wars that will shortly come to pass" (D&C 87:1). He was shown that a civil war would break out in the coming years, which it did, "beginning at the rebellion of South Carolina." He was also shown that warfare would spread throughout the globe, encompassing all nations (D&C 87:1-2). So far we have had two world wars; it is anticipated we will have another. Joseph prophesied it would be warfare that would eventually bring an "end of all nations," making ready the return of the Son of Man (D&C 87:6-8).

When our Lord returns to the earth the second time He will come in glory. He will come as the conqueror of nations much like the Jews expected Him to come the first time. He will subdue all enemies under His feet, cleanse the earth from its wicked inhabitants, and raise the saints to meet Him in the clouds of glory. He will come as the rightful heir of David's throne, the "King of kings, and Lord of lords" (Revelation 19:16; 17:14; 1 Timothy 6:15).[11] All governments will then cease to exist, and both the New Jerusalem and the Jerusalem of old will triumph in glory. The kingdom of God will be established as the earth's government, with Jehovah-Christ its Governor. With the end of all existing governments will come an end to all principle nations, and the earth will return to its former condition of Pangaea. Alas, the great continental puzzle will again be assembled!

The Appointed Time of Christ's Coming

The Second Coming will happen—of this there is no doubt. The question that has been asked through the centuries, however, has been *when*.

---

[11]   Interestingly, Christ is also known as the "King of Saints" (Revelation 15:3).

When will the great and dreadful day occur? The apostles of old asked the same question (Matthew 24:3) to which the Savior replied that not even the angels of heaven know the blessed day, "but my Father only" (Matthew 24:36; JS-Matthew 1:40). Countless voices have been raised throughout the ages predicting the year, and some, the very day when Christ would come. Of such false cries the Prophet Joseph Smith said: "Jesus Christ never did reveal to any man the precise time that He would come." The Prophet admonished, "Go and read the Scriptures, and you cannot find anything that specifies the exact hour He would come; and all that say so are false teachers."[12] If not even the angels know the hour of Christ's return, then why would mortal man? Elder Bruce R. McConkie said of this: "He [the Savior] knows the set time and so does his Father. Perhaps a latter-day prophet will hear the Divine Voice on the day the veil parts and the heavens roll together as a scroll. But there is this difference between his two comings: The fixed and known time of his triumphal return has not been and will not be revealed until the set hour and the fixed time and the very day arrives."[13] Of the fixed time of the Second Coming, Elder McConkie further explained:

> The time for the Second Coming of Christ is as fixed and certain as was the hour of his birth. It will not vary as much as a single second from the divine decree. He will come at the appointed time. The Millennium will not be ushered in prematurely because men turn to righteousness, nor will it be delayed because iniquity abounds. Nephi was able to state with absolute certainty that the God of Israel would come in "six hundred years from the time my father left Jerusalem." (1 Nephi 19:8.) To a later Nephi the Divine Voice acclaimed: "The time is at hand, and on this night shall the

---

12   *TPJS*, p. 341.
13   *The Millennial Messiah*, p. 26.

sign be given, and on the morrow come I into the world." (3 Nephi 1:13.) So shall it be with his return.[14]

Although we do not know the exact year the Savior will make His appearance, we can rest in the knowledge that "the Lord God will do nothing, but he revealeth his secret unto his servants the prophets" (Amos 3:7).[15] It is this author's belief that our prophet-leader will know, if not the exact hour, at least the general time frame of our Lord's return. We can also know the general time period of the Second Coming if we are attuned to the Spirit and to scriptural understanding. Turning again to the words of Elder McConkie: "We know when Christ will come in the clouds of glory, attended by angelic hosts, to be with men on earth again—not the day or the hour, or even the month or the year, but we do know the generation."[16] All the signs that point to the Second Coming affirm that it is *this generation* in which the blessed event will occur.

America will soon see a new political force that will envelop not only this continent, but also the whole world for that matter. As discussed in the previous chapter, it will be a theocracy. Hail the day, Jesus Christ of Nazareth will soon come! "He which testifieth these things saith, Surely I come quickly. Amen. Even so, come, Lord Jesus" (Revelation 22:20).

A Great Day for the Righteous

Although the world we live in is preparing its own requiem mass, the righteous need not fear, for the true saints of God are preparing for the Hallelujah chorus when the great millennium will be ushered in. To the

---

14 Ibid.
15 The Joseph Smith Translation renders this passage, "Surely the Lord God will do nothing *until* he revealeth his secret unto his servants the prophets" (JST Amos 3:7).
16 *The Millennial Messiah*, p. 4.

righteous the last days should not be perceived as days of trial and tear only. In 1990 Bishop Glenn Pace told the saints, "There is no room in the kingdom for fatalism."[17] Many glorious things are to transpire before the Savior's return. The Prophet Joseph Smith elaborated on this theme, saying:

> It is a theme upon which prophets, priests and kings have dwelt with peculiar delight; they have looked forward with joyful anticipation to the day in which we live; and fired with heavenly and joyful anticipation they have sung and written and prophesied of this our day. But they died without the sight. We are the favored people that God has made choice of to bring about the latter-day glory—'the dispensation of the fullness of times when God will gather together all things that are in heaven and all things that are upon the earth, even in one'; when the Saints of God will be gathered in one from every nation, and kindred, and people, and tongue, when Jews will be gathered together into one, the wicked will be gathered together to be destroyed as spoken of by the prophets; the Spirit of God will also dwell with his people, and be withdrawn from the rest of the nations, and all things whether in heaven or on earth will be in one, even in Christ.
>
> The heavenly Priesthood will unite with the earthly to bring about those great purposes; and whilst we are thus united in one common cause, to roll forth the Kingdom of God, the heavenly Priesthood are not idle spectators.
>
> The Spirit of God will be showered down from above, and it will dwell in our midst. The blessings of the Most High will rest upon our tabernacles and our name will be handed down to future ages. Our children will rise up and call us blessed, and generations yet unborn will dwell with peculiar delight upon the scenes that we have passed through—the privations that we have endured, the

---

17   *CR* October 1990.

untiring zeal that we have manifested, the all but insurmountable difficulties that we have overcome in laying the foundation of a work that brought about the glory and blessing which they will realize; a work that God and angels have contemplated with delight for generations past; that fired the souls of the ancient patriarchs and prophets; a work that is destined to bring about the destruction of the powers of darkness, the renovation of the earth, the glory of God and the salvation of the human family.[18]

Although the Prophet undoubtedly spoke concerning the restoration of the gospel and the marvelous work the pioneering fathers would make in furthering the kingdom, he also referenced his comments to our day and the approaching millennial time of rest and renewal when all things will be gathered together in one, even in Christ.

Thus while we sorrow at the tragedies of the daily news, we should also mark with joy the wonderful advancements the Church is making in preparation for the Savior's return: the mass construction of latter-day temples, the more than fifty thousand full-time missionaries in all parts of the world, and the explicitly high convert rate that increases each year. All this *preparatory work* (D&C 78:13) tells of a day not-too-distant when a great priesthood conference will be held at Adam-ondi-Ahman (see D&C 78:15-16). It is there where righteous priesthood holders from all dispensations will meet, and Adam will report to Christ and "Our Lord will then assume the reigns of government"[19]

Indeed we do live in times of joyful anticipation: the hour of our Lord's return is nigh. Let us remember that, as Malachi said, it is a "great day" for the righteous and the God-fearing, but it is a "dreadful day" for the unrepentant and ungodly (Malachi 4:5). To the Saints and good people everywhere the triumphant hymn is this:

---

18   As quoted in *Prophecy and Modern Time's*, p. 10.
19   Joseph Fielding Smith, as quoted in *Prophecy and Modern Time's*, p. 52.

Now let us rejoice in the day of salvation.
*   *   *   *   *

We'll love one another and never dissemble,
But cease to do evil and ever be one.
And when the ungodly are fearing and tremble,
We'll watch for the day when the Savior will come,
*   *   *   *   *

Then all that was promised the Saints will be given,
And they will be crowned with the angels of heav'n,
And earth will appear as the Garden of Eden,
And Christ and his people will ever be one.[20]

Preparing for the Second Coming

The doctrinal treatise of this chapter would fail if something were not written concerning *preparation* for the days to come. Certainly the best way for any of us to prepare for the coming of Christ is to live Christ-like lives. Keeping the commandments, staying true to covenants, and serving others are indeed the crucial pillars of such readiness. Yet there are other duties that appendage to these basic responsibilities. For instance, an ample supply of food storage and other commodities are crucial survival needs. Such readiness has been taught numerous times by prophets and apostles since the restoration. For instance, President Ezra Taft Benson taught: "The revelation to produce and store food may be as essential to our temporal welfare today as boarding the ark was to the people in the days of Noah."[21] Elder McConkie warned in 1979:

---

[20]   *Hymns of The Church of Jesus Christ of Latter-day Saints, # 3.*
[21]   *TETB*, p. 266.

> I stand before the Church this day and raise the warning voice. It is a prophetic voice, for I shall say only what the apostles and prophets have spoken concerning our day…. It is a voice calling upon the Lord's people to prepare for the troubles and desolations which are about to be poured out upon the world without measure. For the moment we live in a day of peace and prosperity but it shall not ever be thus. Great trials lie ahead. All of the sorrows and perils of the past are but a foretaste of what is yet to be. And we must prepare ourselves temporally and spiritually.[22]

Obviously each individual needs to examine one's self to see what preparations need to be made. Each family needs to take inventory to see what improvements should be obtained. As the Lord said in the Doctrine and Covenants, "If ye are prepared ye shall not fear" (D&C 38:30).[23]

There are countless junctions given by the Lord in the scriptures to "Prepare ye, prepare for that which is to come, for the Lord is nigh" (D&C 1:12). Some of the most poignant scriptural warnings concerning the last days are found in the Doctrine and Covenants. These admonitions by the Lord Himself tell us to prepare for the days of tribulation and desolation which are to come (D&C 29:8); to prepare the way of the Lord (33:10), for the great day of the Lord (43:20). The saints are to prepare the supper of the Lamb, to make ready for the coming of the Bridegroom (65:3), for the coming of the Lord (84:28), and against the day of vengeance and burning (85:3), the hour of judgement (88:84; 88:92; 109:38), and for the revelation which is to come (101:23). We need to prepare for the time

---

22 As quoted in *Spiritual Survival in the Last Days*, p. 49.

23 It has been sad that the simple things are what matter most. This is true with regard to the days of preparation. Some of the Lord's most important instructions on preparing for the Second Coming are the *simple, everyday things*, like reading the scriptures, having family prayer, paying a full tithe, getting our homes in order, setting relationship right, attending the temple. Such *simple things* are at the heart of the matter and have eternal value.

when the Lord shall dwell with us (104:59). Section 133 of the Doctrine and Covenants alone is explicit in the warning to prepare for the Second Coming. Said the Lord to His prophet in 1831:

> HEARKEN, O ye people of my church, saith the Lord your God, and hear the word of the Lord concerning you—
>
> The Lord who shall suddenly come to his temple; the Lord who shall come down upon the world with a curse to judgment; yea, upon all the nations that forget God, and upon all the ungodly among you.
>
> For he shall make bare his holy arm in the eyes of all the nations, and all the ends of the earth shall see the salvation of their God.
>
> Wherefore, prepare ye, prepare ye, O my people; sanctify yourselves; gather ye together, O ye people of my church, upon the land of Zion, all you that have not been commanded to tarry.
>
> Go ye out from Babylon. Be ye clean that bear the vessels of the Lord.
>
> Call your solemn assemblies, and speak often one to another. And let every man call upon the name of the Lord.
>
> Yea, verily I say unto you again, the time has come when the voice of the Lord is unto you: Go ye out of Babylon; gather ye out from among the nations, from the four winds, from one end of heaven to the other.
>
> Send forth the elders of my church unto the nations which are afar off; unto the islands of the sea; send forth unto foreign lands; call upon all nations, first upon the Gentiles, and then upon the Jews.
>
> And behold, and lo, this shall be their cry, and the voice of the Lord unto all people: Go ye forth unto the land of Zion, that the borders of my people my be enlarged, and that her stakes may be strengthened, and that Zion may go forth unto the regions round about.

Yea, let the cry go forth among all people: Awake and arise and go forth to meet the Bridegroom; behold and lo, the Bridegroom cometh; go ye out to meet him. Prepare yourselves for the great day of the Lord.

Watch, therefore, for ye know neither the day nor the hour....

For behold, the Lord God hath sent forth the angel crying through the midst of heaven, saying: Prepare ye the way of the Lord, and make his paths straight, for the hour of his coming is nigh— (verses 1-11, 17).

There are two distinct things the Lord has commanded us concerning His coming: The first is to "watch," and the second is to be "ready." The Lord also has said, it is he that "look[s] for me" who "shall see me in the clouds of heaven, clothed with power and great glory." But "he that watches not for me shall be cut off" (D&C 45:44). "Watch, therefore, that ye may be ready. Even so. Amen." (D&C 50:46) "Behold, I come quickly," said the Lord to his servant John, "hold that fast which thou hast, that no man take thy crown" (Revelation 3:11; see also Rev. 22:20; D&C 49:28).

May we all both watch and be ready for the day in which the Son of God returns. May we put our trust in Him who saves and follow His Guiding Spirit. "I know there are difficult days ahead," said Ezra Taft Benson, "politically, economically, socially, and spiritually. But God rules this world. He is at the helm. May he help us to be prepared for any eventuality."[24] Truly "If [we] are prepared, [we] shall not fear" (D&C 38:30).

---

24   *So Shall Ye Reap,* p. 195.

11

The Integrity of America

Integrity, where art thou?
Wait! I see thee now:
Thou art in the humble life.

—James Leroux

The integrity of the upright shall guide them:
But the perverseness of transgressors shall destroy them.

—Proverbs 11:3

As has been stated in the preface of this book, I love America, the country of my birth. I am eternally grateful to Omnipotence for allowing me, even blessing me to live here.

I am grateful for the Book of Mormon, the greatest American book ever written.

I am grateful for the American flag and its sacred symbolism.

I am grateful for a Constitution that safeguards my individual rights.

I am thankful for free speech and the freedom to worship.

I could continue recounting thanks for the myriad blessings I have been given. In doing so I would have to admit that much of what has been given me has been made available through living in a free society. A whole book would not suffice to recount all my blessings and the thanks I feel for them. Let it be said, however, that I am grateful for the good and the honorable people of America, for those citizens who respect and love their country, their freedoms, and their neighbors.

America's Integrity—Past, Present and Future

Through the medium of this book we have constructed our own time machine, and together we have traveled certain epochs of America's past, present, and future. Truly we have seen her in three distinct perspectives. Hopefully these different perspectives have given us a keener understanding of our noble land. If we view America in her proper light—through correct doctrinal understanding—then we must view her being endowed with much integrity. Concerning this theme, President George Q. Cannon taught in 1856 that "the Fathers of the Republic were confident in the integrity of their own motives, and were satisfied as to the propriety of establishing such a form of government." But the Founders knew they were laying only the foundation; "they were fully aware that its success and perpetuity depended, altogether, on the *integrity* and correct deportment of the people."[1] President Gordon B. Hinckley has said: "*No nation can either become or remain great if there is an absence of integrity in its citizens.*"[2]

Elder Joseph B. Wirthlin explained the meaning of integrity. "Integrity," he said, is "a firm adherence to the highest moral and ethical standards." He also taught that integrity "is essential to the life of a true

---

1   *Gospel Truth*, p. 540.
2   *TGBH*, p. 267.

Latter-day Saint."[3] And Elder Marvin J. Ashton taught: "Integrity must be the foundation of moral life."[4]

There is no doubt that we have lost some of our greatness as a nation. Using an old cliché, the Founding Fathers would probably roll over in their graves if they knew some of the things that go on in the nation today. Surely they must know. And it doesn't take an Albert Einstein to discern the sad facts that the United States is now suffering the effects of secularism and mass spiritual degeneracy. As I see it, America has to pass through three phases of growth and decline before her millennial time of rest and renewal. Let me explain the phases: 1) Founding, colonization, and democratic triumph. 2) Scientific and technological growth, world power and prestige, and a secular stream of free speech patterns, and a turning away from old-time values. 3) Chaotic structure in government, internal and international warfare, and a total separation from religious tenets. These phases, mind you, are only a breakdown of how *I see* the destiny of America. Some of the phases overlap. According to this reasoning we are now living in the latter part of the second phase. This bespeaks that the third phase is rapidly approaching. It also warns of the telling theme of the last days—indeed, the Second Coming of Christ is near, "even at the doors" (See Matthew 24:33; Mark 13:29; D&C 110:16; JS-Matthew 1:39).

The prophecies of the last days fill many of us with emotion, uncertainty, and fear. Maybe these feelings arise because we are not as prepared as we could be, or even should be. Perhaps these feelings come because we are not certain what role we play in God's divine drama. Or maybe it's because we do not understand the prophecies well enough to view them other than with fear and dread. But whatever the reason, know this: God is at the helm. It is for each of us to put our trust in the Lord that He may direct our path, that we may feel His presence and influence in our lives— His quiet guiding Spirit. "The challenge before us in this critical time of

---

3   *CR* April 1990, p. 38.
4   *The Measure of Our Hearts*, p. 73.

the world's history," said Elder Ezra Taft Benson, "is probably without an equal."[5] We read in Church history and in American history and marvel with gratitude at the integrity of our noble forefathers. Yet we must remember that we are making history today. What kind of legacy will we, both as individuals and as a nation, leave for future generations?

It is for each of us to prioritize and to maximize our integrity, to carry on the legacy that our forefathers have left to us, to stand tall and be counted worthy to stand when the Savior does come. It is time for us as individuals and as families to make serious goals and aspire to them with full purpose of heart. It is time to reflect on the past, learn from the present, and face the future with courage and conviction. Indeed it is time to be people of integrity, to stand fast in that liberty whereby God has made us free.

I firmly believe that despite the turmoil and strife we hear about so often, America is essentially good. There is much integrity in American soil. There is much integrity in the American business. There is much integrity in the American family, just as there is much integrity in many American citizens. There is much integrity to be found in America's past and present. And there will be integrity for the future! Just look at our noble sons and daughters!

May integrity be your motto and mine as it was for Job: "till I die I will not remove mine integrity from me" (Job 27:5). Come what may, the Psalmist said, "But as for me, I will walk in mine integrity" (Ps. 26:11).

God bless America, land that I love—!

---

5   *So Shall Ye Reap*, p. 157.

Afterword

Songs can be inspirational and even reverential at times. In the Doctrine & Covenants the Lord told Emma Smith that the song of the righteous is as a prayer unto Him (D&C 25:12). America has been blessed with a floodtide legacy of patriotic songs that are as a prayer *for* her. Such songs, written by able and penitent individuals possessed of rare talent, have blessed the United States with honor, nobility, and deep patriotism. For me, emotions run high whenever I hear our national anthem sung with dignity and conviction. I also feel emotional when I hear the dignifying *America the Beautiful*. It is a beautiful song in itself, and I would like to include it as the conclusion to my book. The song's real power, however, comes from singing it (and hearing it) and not reading it only. Thus I hope when you read these inspirational words that you will not help yourself but to sing them!

Oh, beautiful for spacious skies, For amber waves of grain,
For purple mountain majesties Above the fruited plain!
America! America! God shed his grace on thee,
And crown thy good with brotherhood From sea to shining sea.

Oh, beautiful for pilgrim feet, Whose stern, impassioned stress
A thoroughfare of freedom beat Across the wilderness!
America! America! God mend thine ev'ry flaw,
Confirm thy soul in self-control, Thy liberty in law.

Oh, beautiful for heroes proved In liberating strife,
Who more than self their country loved, And mercy more than life!
America! America! May God thy gold refine,
Till all success be nobleness, And ev'ry gain divine.

Oh, beautiful for patriot dream That sees beyond the years
Thine alabaster cities gleam, Undimmed by human tears!
America! America! God shed his grace on thee,
And crown thy good with brotherhood From sea to shining sea.

—Katherine Lee Bates, 1859-1929

About the Author

Andrew S. Weeks, a native of southern California, is a convert to The Church of Jesus Christ of Latter-day Saints. In the Church Brother Weeks has served in numerous positions, including having served two years as a missionary to Oklahoma. Andy is the author of numerous short stories of fiction and nonfiction content. He is also a writer of poetry, and in 1998 he was a semifinalist in a national poetry competition. He is currently a student of journalism at a popular university. He is married to the former Heidi Snyder, and they have one son. *America in Perspective* is Andy's first book.

Bibliography

Andersen, H. Verlan.   *The Great and Abominable Church of the Devil.*
Orem, UT: SunRise Publishers, 1972.

Ashton, Marvin J.   *The Measure of Our Hearts.*
Salt Lake City: Deseret Book, 1991.

Balmforth, David N.   *America's Coming Crisis: Prophetic Warnings, Divine Destiny.*
Bountiful, UT: Horizon Publishers, 1998.

Benson, Ezra Taft.   *An Enemy Hath Done This.*
Salt Lake City: Parliament Publishers, 1969.

Benson, Ezra Taft.   *Come, Listen to a Prophets Voice.*
Salt Lake City: Deseret Book, 1990.

Benson, Ezra Taft.   *God, Family, Country: Our Three Great Loyalties.*
Salt Lake City: Deseret Book, 1974.

Benson, Ezra Taft.   *The Constitution: A Heavenly Banner.*
Salt Lake City: Deseret Book,1986.

Benson, Ezra Taft.   *The Red Carpet: Socialism—The Royal Road to Communism.*
Salt Lake City: Bookcraft, 1962.

Benson, Ezra Taft.   *The Teachings of Ezra Taft Benson.*
                            Salt Lake City: Bookcraft, 1988.

Benson, Ezra Taft.   *This Nation Shall Endure.*
                            Salt Lake City: Deseret Book, 1979.

Benson, Ezra Taft.   *So Shall Ye Reap.*
                            Salt Lake City: Deseret Book, 1960.

Brewster, Hoyt W.   *Behold, I Come Quickly.*
                            Salt Lake City: Deseret Book, 1994.

Burton, Alma P., comp.   *Discourses of the Prophet Joseph Smith.*
                            Salt Lake City: Deseret Book, 1977.

Burton, Alma P.   *Doctrines of the Prophets.*
                            Springville, UT: Cedar Fort, Inc., 1994.

Cannon, George Q.   *Gospel Truth.*
                            Salt Lake City: Deseret Book, 1987.

Carothers, Thomas.   "Democracy Without Illusions"
                            Foreign Affairs, Jan/Feb 1997.

Conference Report   The Church of Jesus Christ of Latter-day Saints.
                            Salt Lake City: October 1939.

Conference Report   The Church of Jesus Christ of Latter-day Saints.
                            Salt Lake City: April 1948.

Conference Report   The Church of Jesus Christ of Latter-day Saints.
                            Salt Lake City: April 1963.

Conference Report   The Church of Jesus Christ of Latter-day Saints.
                            Salt Lake City: April 1990.

Crowther, Duane S.   *America: God's Chosen Land of Liberty.*
                            Bountiful, UT: Horizon Publishers, 1987.

Crowther, Duane S.   *Prophecy—Key to the Future*, revised edition.
                            Bountiful, UT: Horizon Publishers, 1996.

De Tocqueville, Alexis.   *Democracy in America.*
Ed. Richard D. Heffner.
New York: New American Library, 1956.

Encyclopedia Americana.   Danbury, CT: Grolier Incorporated, 1998.

Evans, Richard L.   *Richard Evans' Quote Book.*
Salt Lake City: Publishers Press,1971.

Families. Compilation.   Salt Lake City: Deseret Book, 1994.

Featherstone, Vaughn J.   *More Purity Give Me.*
Salt Lake City: Deseret Book, 1991.

"God Isn't Dead."   The Salt Lake Tribune, December 28, 1998.

Grant, Heber J.   *Gospel Standards,*12th edition.
Salt Lake City: Deseret News Press, 1969.

Hales, Robert E.   *Secret Combinations Today: A Voice of Warning.*
Bountiful, UT: Horizon Publishers, 1996.

"Hatch Again Pushes
Amendment To Prohibit
Burning of the Flag."   The Salt Lake Tribune, February 5, 1998.

Hinckley, Bryant S.   *Sermons and Missionary Services of Melvin Joseph Ballard.*
Deseret Book, 1949.

Hinckley, Gordon B.   *Teachings of Gordon B. Hinckley.*
Salt Lake City: Deseret Book, 1997.

Hymns   The Church of Jesus Christ of Latter-day Saints.
Salt Lake City: 1985.

"I Am Not a UN Soldier."   *The New American*, October 2, 1995.

"Inspiration: How U.S.
Anthem Was Born."   The Salt Lake Tribune, December 6, 1998.

Internationalism:
Opposing Viewpoints.   St. Paul, Minn: Greenhaven Press, Inc., 1985.

Isolationism:
Opposing Viewpoints.   San Diego, CA: Greenhaven Press, Inc., 1995.

Josephus, Flavius.   *Antiquities of the Jews* as contained in
                            The Complete Works of Flavius Josephus.
                            Translated by Wm. Winston.
                            Grand Rapids, MI: Kregel Publications, 1960.

Journal of Discourses   London, England: Latter-day Saints' Book
                                 Depot, 26 volumes 1854-1886.

Kimball, Spencer W.   *The Teachings of Spencer W. Kimball.*
                             Salt Lake City: Bookcraft, 1982.

Lee, Harold B.   *The Teachings of Harold B. Lee,*
                        edited by Clyde J. Williams.
                        Salt Lake City: Bookcraft, 1996.

Lee, Robert W.   *The United Nations Conspiracy.*
                        Belmont, MS: Western Islands, 1981.

Liechty, Jay.   *America's State Church.*
                       USA: Calder Press, Inc., 1995.

Loeb, Aaron, ed.   *The Wit & Wisdom of Mark Twain.*
                          New York: Barnes & Noble Books, 1996.

Lucas, James W.   *Working Toward Zion: Principles of the United*
and Warner P. Woodworth.   *Order for the Modern World.*
                                  Salt Lake City: Aspen Books, 1996.

Maxwell, Neal A.   *Not My Will, But Thine.*
                          Salt Lake City: Bookcraft, 1988.

McConkie, Bruce R.   *Doctrinal New Testament Commentary,*
                            Volume III.
                            Salt Lake City: Bookcraft, 1973.

McConkie, Bruce R. comp.   *Doctrines of Salvation: Sermons and Writings of Joseph Fielding Smith.*
Salt Lake City: Bookcraft, 1954.

McConkie, Bruce R.   *Mormon Doctrine*, 2d edition.
Salt Lake City: Bookcraft, 1966.

McConkie, Bruce R.   *The Millennial Messiah: The Second Coming of the Son of Man.*
Salt Lake City: Deseret Book, 1982.

McConkie, Joseph Fielding.   *Here We Stand.*
Salt Lake City: Deseret Book, 1995.

McConkie, Joseph Fielding and Robert L. Millet.   *The Man Adam.*
Salt Lake City: Bookcraft, 1990.

McKay, David O.   *Gospel Ideals.*
Salt Lake City: Deseret Book, 1953.

McKay, David O.   *Man May Know for Himself.*
Salt Lake City: Deseret Book, 1967.

Michener, James A.   *This Noble Land: My Vision for America.*
New York: Random House, 1996.

Morrison, Alexander B.   *Zion—A Light in the Darkness.*
Salt Lake City: Deseret Book, 1997.

Moyers, Bill.   *A World of Ideas: Conversations with thoughtful men and women about American life today and the ideas shaping our future.*
New York: Doubleday, 1989.

Newquist, Jerreld L.   *Prophets, Principles and National Survival.*
Salt Lake City: Publishers Press, 1964.

Nibley, Hugh.   *Of All Things,* 2d edition.
Salt Lake City: Deseret Book, 1993.

Packer, Boyd K.   *Let Not Your Heart Be Troubled.*
Salt Lake City: Bookcraft, 1991.

Pratt, Orson.   *Orson Pratt's Works.*
                                 Salt Lake City: Deseret News Press, 1945.

Pratt, Parley P.   *The Voice of Warning.*
                                 London: Latter-day Saints' Book Depot, 1871.

Schlesinger, Jr. Arthur.   "Has Democracy a Future?"
                                 Foreign Affairs, Sep/Oct 1997.

Skousen, W. Cleon.   *Prophecy and Modern Times.*
                                 Salt Lake City: Ensign Publishers, 1939.

Skousen, W. Cleon.   *The Naked Communist,* 3d edition.
                                 Salt Lake City: Ensign Publishers, 1960.

Smith, Mark A.   *The Power of God.* Bountiful,
                                 UT: Horizon Publishers, 1997.

Smith, Joseph.   *History of the Church,* 7 volumes.
                                 Salt Lake City: Deseret Book, 1948-1950
                                 edition.

Smith, Joseph F.   *Gospel Doctrine.*
                                 Salt Lake City: Deseret Book, 1986 edition.

Smith, Joseph Fielding.   *Answers to Gospel Questions,* 5 volumes.
                                 Salt Lake City: Deseret Book, 1957-1966.

Smith, Joseph Fielding.   *The Pathway to Perfection.*
                                 Salt Lake City: Deseret Book, 1985.

Smith, Joseph Fielding, comp.   *Teachings of the Prophet Joseph Smith.*
                                 Salt lake City: Deseret Book, 1976.

Spirit of America, The.   Salt Lake City: Bookcraft, 1998.

Stephenson Jr., D. Grier,   *American Government,* 2d edition.
Robert J. Bresler,   New York: HarperCollins Publishers, 1992.
Robert J. Friedrich and
Joseph J. Karlesky.

Talbott, Strobe "Democracy and the National Interest"
Foreign Affairs, Nov/Dec 1996.

Taylor, John. *The Gospel Kingdom: Writings and Discourses of John Taylor.*
Salt Lake City: Bookcraft, 1987.

Widtsoe, John A. comp. *The Discourses of Brigham Young.*
Salt Lake City: Deseret Book, 1954.

Williams, Clyde J., ed. *The Teachings of Howard W. Hunter.*
Salt Lake City: Bookcraft, 1997.

Williams, Clyde J., ed. *The Teachings of George Albert Smith.*
Salt Lake City: Bookcraft, 1996.

Williams, Clyde J., ed. *The Teachings of Lorenzo Snow.*
Salt Lake City: Bookcraft, 1996.

Woodruff, Wilford. *The Discourses of Wilford Woodruff.*
Salt Lake City: Bookcraft, 1946.

Woods, Harold & Geraldine. *The United Nations.*
New York: Grolier, 1985.

Yorgason, Blain & Brenton. *Spiritual Survival in the Last Days.*
Salt Lake City: Deseret Book, 1990.